THE AD MAKERS

531913

This book is to be returned on or before the last date stamped below.

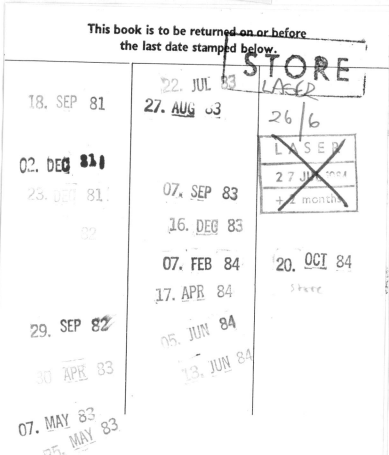

STORE

18. SEP 81	22. JUL 83	LASER
	27. AUG 83	26/6
02. DEC 81		LASER
23. DEC 81	07. SEP 83	27 JU 1984
82	16. DEC 83	+ 1 month
	07. FEB 84	20. OCT 84
	17. APR 84	Store
29. SEP 82	05. JUN 84	
30 APR 83	13. JUN 84	
07. MAY 83		
25. MAY 83		

The Ad Makers

Winston Fletcher

LONDON

MICHAEL JOSEPH

To Pig

First published in Great Britain by
MICHAEL JOSEPH LTD
52 Bedford Square
London W.C.1
1973

ISBN 0 7181 1118 4

Set and Printed in Great Britain by
Northumberland Press Limited, Gateshead
in Georgian eleven on twelve point
and bound by James Burn at Esher, Surrey

CONTENTS

INTRODUCTION

This book started out as a joint venture with David Abbott. We were both thirty-three, and Managing Directors of two London advertising agencies. The book was to be called, modestly, 'How to be a Success in Advertising by the age of 33', and we produced a detailed synopsis of the contents. Somehow the venture never materialized. That's the thing about admen's schemes: they never quite come off as planned.

Nonetheless I am extremely grateful to David for having got me started; also to Oliver Stutchbury for having told me where to put my adverbs; to Alan Smith, for telling me in one succinct sentence what was wrong with the first draft; to Len Deighton, for the close personal interest he took in the story relating to himself; to Jackie Pritchard for typing, re-typing and re-re-typing many of the chapters; and to my wife both for designing the cover and for so often thinking of the apposite word when I was stumped.

Parts of the book have previously appeared in my articles in *Campaign*, *New Society*, the *Director* and the *Financial Times*—but most of it is New! Each of the chapters deals with one particular aspect of advertising agency life, and so the book is structured as a series of episodic, pointilliste, essays. But the whole is intended to be at least a little greater than the sum of its parts.

If I have seemed to concentrate too much upon the bungles and bloomers we Ad Makers make, this is because I happen to see the world, history, progress, Life itself, as a concatenation of mostly accidental events—events over which human beings have far less control than they like to believe. The Ad Makers are neither more nor less incompetent on average than everyone else. Prediction, power and achievement are matters of odds rather than certainties. Great men are right rather more often, the rest of us rather less.

Nevertheless the specific mishaps which Ad Makers are

heir to spring from the specific nature of the advertising business. I happen to find it an endlessly entertaining, curious, stimulating and worthwhile way to make a living. I hope that is what I have communicated.

1   Like That's the Agency Scene

We used to have an Eskimo client. He was called Dennis Ing, and he was a group product manager at International Distillers and Vintners. Rumour had it that he had come to IDV from J. Lyons and Co. because there they had put him in charge of ice cream. Presumably Lyons' computer staff-selection programme had diligently studied his curriculum vitae. Dennis, the story went, had walked out in anger.

Perhaps as a result of his ancestry, Dennis was no typical grey-flannel-suited-large-company-executive. His flamboyant check suits, black shirts and bright wide ties clearly distinguished him from his colleagues in the executives' washroom. His reading habits and his interest in the arts were catholic; his attitudes to politics revolutionary.

At IDV, where he was our client, he was responsible for Justina Wines. We were very proud of having what we were certain was the only Eskimo client in London. It seemed particularly appropriate that an Eskimo should have control over the innumerable bottles of Portuguese table-wine going into suburban British homes each year.

In 1970 IDV ran an exceptionally successful sales conference at the Excelsior Hotel, London Airport. It was unlike any other sales conference I have attended, which is a fair number. When the sales reps flew in from the far corners of the British Isles they were ushered into a large hall in which had been built a mock fairground of stalls and side-shows. But bingo, swing boats and bumper cars, were there none. Instead each stall promoted one of IDV's products. There was a kind of ghost-train-cum-maze for Smirnoff Vodka—as the salesmen groped their way through it they were terrified in turn by hanging paper tarantulas, luminously glowing skeletons and next year's advertising plans. There was a mock Victorian

pier for Perrier Water and Lillet Vermouth, complete with
What the Butler Saw machines (next year's advertising plans,
again). There were stalls for Hennessy Cognac and Croft
Sherries, for Gilbeys Gin and J & B Rare and Bols.

For Justina Wines we had designed a mock cinema. The
salesmen queued up to see a slide show comprising what in
retrospect were not-nearly revealing enough pics of girls drinking Justina; and next year's advertising plans.

The sales conference was to start on a Sunday. On the
previous Friday morning Ian Scott, the agency's account super-
visor on Justina, rushed into my office in panic. As contact
man between the advertising agency and our client IDV he
was responsible for organizing the agency's side of the sales
conference. The last few days before a sales conference always
involve a frenzy of hectic activity, frayed tempers and first-
night nerves.

'Usherettes,' he said.

I looked up from the Goya sales statistics which I had
been unsuccessfully trying to study for two hours. Clients
send their ad agencies sales figures to help them assess the
success or otherwise of the advertising. The sales figures are
rarely much help.

'Usherettes?'

'We've forgotten to get any usherettes.'

'Are you,' I asked, resorting to facetiousness, my mind still
befuddled with sales statistics, 'in desperate need of a choc
ice?'

'For the IDV Product Fair. We'll need two usherettes to
show the reps into their seats and out again.'

'So we will.'

'We've not got any.'

'So we haven't.'

'What should we do?'

I tried to sound calm, wise and reassuring. 'There are bound
to be millions of girls dying to spend Sunday afternoon
pretending to be usherettes at the Excelsior Hotel ... for
money.'

An hour later Ian returned. 'I've got Jayne and Lu. From
the Penthouse.'

'Lu?'

'You know. The girl we used on that Casino Sekt poster.'

'I know. She's fantastic. She's also very black.'

'Yes.'

'Do you think it's all right to have a black usherette at a sales conference?'

'She'll be wonderful. Think how much impact she'll make. She was simply marvellous on that poster. She'll make the Justina stand the most memorable one there. She'll be ... the star of the show.'

'I'm not sure.' It wasn't a problem that had ever occurred to me before. 'Half the bloody reps are bound to come from Smethwick or to be members of the British National Party.'

'Don't be ridiculous.' Having managed to rustle up two very acceptable girls within an hour, Ian had expected congratulations rather than carping questions.

'This isn't our party,' I pointed out. 'It's IDV's party. For *their* salesmen. The question is: do they want a black usherette?'

'Honestly, Lu will be the hit of the show. Apart from anything else, she's got the biggest breasts in the Penthouse. Don't you want the Justina stand to have impact?'

'Lu is nice. She's beautiful. And as you say she's got a more than ample bosom. She's also black, and before you employ her I think you should check with IDV that it's OK. In fact, I think you should check that both Jayne and Lu are OK. That's normal procedure.'

Ian paused and looked at me suspiciously. 'I never expected this from you.'

'It's nothing to do with *my* views. It's not my conference. Reps are notoriously conservative, reactionary and bigoted. You wouldn't send a nun to be an usherette in a synagogue. Not without checking with the rabbi first.'.

'Why should we pander to the reps' hypothetical fascist prejudices? All IDV's top management will adore Lu. She's wonderful.'

'Why take a girl to a party where she's not one hundred per cent welcome? It's not an NAACP rally; it's a sales conference, the purpose of which is to enthuse the salesmen and make their lives a little happier.'

'I really never would have expected this from you,' Ian repeated, now more in genuine sorrow than in anger.

'Look. Just phone Dennis Ing and check. If he says it's OK to bring Lu, it's OK. Just check, that's all.'

'But I can't.'

'Why can't you?'

'How can you ask an Eskimo if he minds us having a black usherette?'

'Dennis'll see the point immediately. If he thinks there's no problem, that's fine. And remember,' I chided him gently, 'in this business you never know where trouble may come from. You need sensitive antennae and the whiskers of a cat.'

Needless to say, Dennis agreed. Lu came to the sales conference, displayed an almost overwhelming expanse of bosom and as Ian had predicted was a great success. Everything seemed to have gone smoothly and beautifully until around midnight when I was sipping my third or fourth large nightcap alone with Dennis in his room at the hotel. 'You know,' he said suddenly, 'on Friday I was going to tell you to fire that shit Ian Scott.'

I choked on my nightcap. Large accounts can be lost if a client dislikes his agency contact man. The client starts to dislike everything the agency does, since it is the contact man who shows it all to him. The contact man starts to dislike the client. Within the agency, people start to say it's a difficult account to work on. All of a sudden the agency learns that the client has an old buddy at J. Walter Thompson and the account is moving. The client phones and whispers a few platitudes about how much he appreciates the fine work the agency has done over the years, but he feels that the time has come for fresh thinking. Maybe £250,000 billing moves, and that's equivalent to five or six people's jobs in an agency. So if things are looking bad—and advertising is not exactly a growth industry these days—five or six people find themselves unemployed. All because the client and the agency contact man had bad chemistry between them, which nobody diagnosed early enough.

'I always thought you liked Ian Scott.'

'Sure I used to like him. I used to like him fine. But it's all over.' Dennis had sipped a few nightcaps himself.

'What happened? I thought the Justina slide show went great.'

'Sure it went great. Everything went great. Except that shit Scott. He's a turd, man. Do you realize he phoned me on Friday to ask if we'd object to Lu? I always knew he was a fucking Tory. Now he's a fucking racialist Tory. That's it. He just needles me too much, man.'

I emptied my glass, and stared at a half-lit Tretchikoff Negress reproduction on the wall. Why, I wondered, is the light in hotel rooms always so yellow? A green Negress bathed in a dim yellow glow. 'I told him to phone you.'

'*You* told him!'

'I thought we should check it out with you first.'

'God, man. I always knew you were a fucking namby-pamby liberal. It's right what the Black Power guys say. It's right. The wishy-washy liberals are the real bastards. At least you know where you are with the Klan.'

'I wasn't against Lu. I just wanted to check that you knew and agreed. Anyway, it wasn't Ian Scott's fault. I made him ask you. We had about an hour's argument. He thought I was wrong, too. Maybe I *was* wrong.'

'Of course you were wrong. Just terribly, terribly wrong. But what would you expect from a half-baked left-wing in-tellectual?'

I slumped back in my armchair. Perhaps my schoolboy morality had been misplaced. Perhaps I should have let Ian Scott take the rap. Ian could always be moved to another account. But could Dennis ever be reconciled to an agency run by a namby-pamby-wishy-washy-half-baked-left-wing-intellectual? I poured myself another large J & B. One of the few good things to be said for sales conferences, I thought, is that the liquor is paid for out of the sales department's budget. 'I suppose it was stupid of me,' I slurred, 'getting Ian to ask an Eskimo whether he'd object to an African.'

'Eskimo? What you talking about, man? You stoned out of your mind already?'

'Making him ask you, I mean. And you being an Eskimo.'

It was as if a small blast of dynamite had exploded. I thought I noticed the Tretchikoff judder. 'Eskimo? Eskimo?' Dennis yelled, 'who says I'm an Eskimo? What shit's putting it around I'm an Eskimo? I'm a Chink, man. A Chink. Can't you see I'm a Chink? You blind?'

A truth that I had felt to be self-evident, an oft-discussed and indisputable fact was being whisked without warning away from me. No longer to be the only advertising agency in London with an Eskimo client seemed a bleak prospect, not to be accepted without a struggle.

'But ... but everyone knows you're an Eskimo. You used to work on Lyons Maid. That's why you left.'

'Who says so? Look, man, I know what I am. I'm a third generation Canadian of Chinese origin. That makes me a Canadian Chink. Not an Eskimo.' Dennis had calmed down now, and was beginning to enjoy the idea of having been believed to be an Eskimo. 'And moreover,' he said thoughtfully, 'if I ever find the guy who's been putting it around I'm an Eskimo, I'll screw his fucking neck off. Man.'

Like that's the agency scene, man. If you're gonna succeed in it, you'll need to be the cat's own whiskers.

2   How to Become a Sorcerer's Apprentice

The devious hidden-persuaders, the faceless, snakily-scheming, power-hungry cat's-whiskers who cunningly and unerringly manipulate our unsuspecting minds, tempting us to buy products we do not want at prices inflated by their exorbitant salaries—these men, not surprisingly, devote a good deal of their crafty brain-power to the selection of their heirs. Each would-be apprentice, before being admitted to the sorcerers' tribe, must expect to undergo the most exquisitely subtle screening techniques; he will be analysed by masters of thought-control, dissected by minds as incisive and remorseless as scalpels.

I am especially well qualified to offer a few words of wisdom on the problems of getting into advertising, having inadvertently entered the business twice.

'Mr. Fletcher,' Stanhope Shelton, then the fiery creative director of Mather and Crowther (now Ogilvy Benson and Mather), popped the question: 'Why do you want to get into advertising?' It was the standard opener, deceptively designed to put me at my ease, so that my guard might drop.

'People,' came my pre-digested reply, 'I'm simply fascinated by people. Love them. Can't get enough of them. And that's what advertising is all about, isn't it? People?'

I was sitting at one end of a huge oval table. In the far distance at the other end of the table sat Shelton with a coven of inscrutable interrogators. He eyed me sternly. 'Is that what they told you to say, at the University Appointments Board?'

I was nonplussed. I had attended many interviews on my way to this final short list, but nobody had previously questioned my standard meaningless answer to the standard pointless question.

'Why didn't you answer truthfully that you're coming into it for the money?'

'I'm not. Not only the money, anyway. You can earn good money lots of other ways.'

'Mr. Fletcher, if I seriously thought that you weren't coming into it for the money I would hesitate to employ you. All of us here,' imperiously he waved his arm, gathering everyone in the room into his sweeping generalization, 'are in it for the money. That's what business is all about. Nothing to be ashamed of. Very right and proper. Why else would we work twelve hours a day, seven days a week?'

Whether or not I was interested only in the money, two weeks after starting work there as a trainee I realized that I wasn't much interested in Mather and Crowther.

There are no guaranteed proven and successful rules for getting into advertising. Some of us get in only after suffering a battery of selection tests; others are lucky enough to be born with a cousin who knows the brother of Someone Important at Young and Rubicam.

Advertising agencies own no machinery, no capital resources, no stocks. The inventory goes down in the lift and home every night. In this respect advertising is no different from any of the traditional professions; they too are manpower-intensive service industries without much capital. Over the years the professions have devised systems of exams which have formalized their staff-recruitment procedures. You become a solicitor or an accountant or a doctor by passing—and only by passing—the relevant exams. There are exams for admen too. Passing them may, unfortunately, get you nowhere. There are formal public exams—set by a body unhappily called the Communication Advertising and Marketing Education Foundation. But many large agencies set their own tests. They have intelligence tests, psychology tests, adaptability tests, creativity tests, personality tests, and probably blood tests and urine tests too. Happily the more esoteric of these tests all seem to be going out of fashion. Their results have proved consistently unreliable, and the young now show an admirable unwillingness to suffer such indignities.

Many agencies do still, however, ask applicants to complete a straightforward general paper. Common questions include (in addition to 'Why do you want to get into advertising?'):

> List three current advertising campaigns you particularly like and say why.

> List three current advertising campaigns you particularly dislike and say why.

> Invent a wholly new product, give it a name and write an advertisement for it.

> Write an advertisement persuading more tourists to visit somewhere you know well.

> A client has asked you to prepare a campaign for a new detergent/cigarette/motor car. List the ten most important questions you would ask him before starting work on it.

> Write an advertisement to sell tinned turnips to either (a) a newly arrived party of Martians or (b) the Yeovil Branch of the Consumerists Against Canned Foods Club.

All requiring the applicant to show effusive enthusiasm and knowledge of advertising before he or she knows very much about it. Which is not unusual. Most industrial companies believe a deep-felt vocational involvement in one's job to be highly desirable, if not vital. When I was applying for a job as a ladies' shoe salesman in Toronto the shop manager quizzed me at length to uncover the extent of my real, genuine, warm-hearted passion for feet.

'They're bound to ask you,' I had been warned again and again, 'why you want to get into advertising.'

'I haven't the least idea.'

'That won't get you a job in an advertising agency,' the

University Appointments Board man would reprimand me sternly, the intonation of his voice implying that a job in an advertising agency was on a par at the very least with being Tsar of all the Russias.

There are a few rare curiously dedicated people who decide at an early age that advertising is to be their bag. I have interviewed students who could name the top twenty agencies in London and list their accounts; interviewed schoolboys who apparently had been designing posters while they were in nappies; interviewed graduates who had been rejected by forty agencies but who were still filled with determination to get into the business. Robin Wight, now at twenty-seven the creative director of Euro Advertising, author of *The Day The Pigs Refused To Be Driven To Market** and winner of innumerable advertising awards, decided during his first year at Cambridge that advertising was to be the great passion of his life. While still at university he started his own advertising agency and achieved early fame when a profile called 'Undergradman' was published in the *Guardian*. By the time he left Cambridge he had been offered jobs at extraordinary salaries by several of London's leading agencies. He became a creative director at the age of twenty-four. He can name the writers and artists working on just about every important account in town, and talking to him one sometimes feels that his fanatical enthusiasm for his chosen career borders on being amiably dotty. Possibly Robin is the reason why many interviewers still attach such importance to asking: 'Why do you want to get into advertising?'

It has always seemed daft to me. Notwithstanding the exceptions, the great majority of 15- to 20-year-olds end up in the jobs they end up in by accident. Because mum always wanted them to be an airline pilot. Because they saw a play on television in which the vet pulled a lot of birds. Not because they had decided to make a career as a freelance spinach grower at the age of three and their ambition had never wavered. For me, advertising was very much a fourth choice. Given the option I would have much preferred a

---

* 1972, Granada Publishing.

career as President of the United States, as a Brilliant and Successful Novelist, or—at the very worst—as The Richest Man in the World.

If you want to get into advertising today it is all but essential to have acquired a degree of some sort. This requirement is partly the result of the widespread view that almost anyone who can accurately spell his or her own name can find a place in university nowadays; and partly due to agency selection boards' very right and proper uncertainty concerning their own abilities to select. They modestly feel that there is an element of at least partial safety in recruiting people with initials after their surnames as well as before. Having been to Oxford or Cambridge is, not surprisingly, best of all.

While still at Cambridge, I was interviewed by Michael English, now chairman of Hobson Bates and Partners—one of the most successful agencies in London. He was then responsible for graduate recruitment at the London Press Exchange, since taken over by Leo Burnett Inc. of Chicago.

My interview with Michael English went perfectly. Like most other undergraduates entering advertising, I was concerned as to its morality and as to what would happen to my soul. I had heard that one would suffer agonies of guilt, with only £2,000 a year and a duodenal ulcer by the age of twenty-eight as solace. English reassured me that none of these need be my fate, and put me on his short list for the LPE's final selection.

The next interview was in London with an LPE director, and as soon as we met I knew that he was the kind of man I liked and could get on with. It so happened that his daughter had just left Cambridge too. Unfortunately she had not done well in her Finals, and he was disappointed. For about half an hour he quizzed me about her poor results. Did I think she wasn't clever enough? Hadn't she worked hard enough? Did she spend too much time going out with too many young men? Hardly knowing the girl, the questions were difficult to answer, and I said so. Nevertheless, although it was taking rather an unusual course, I sensed that the interview was going well and that he was artfully using the discussion to assess my intellectual fibre and was slyly peering deep into my soul.

'That,' I thought to myself with pleasure, going down in the lift afterwards, 'is the advantage of going to Cambridge. Before you went to Cambridge you had difficulty with the local television dealer's daughter because her dad thought you were too poor to be respectable. Like they say, it's not *what* you know, it's *who* you know. Good old Cambridge. That's the way to get jobs.'

Two weeks later I received the rudest rejection letter I've ever had. Most rejection letters say you're wonderful ... but not quite right. This one bluntly said I was quite wrong.

I noticed a Box Number advertisement in *The Times* Personal Column offering a career in advertising to any brilliant graduate with a First or who felt he should have got a First. I qualified in the latter category. The reply offering me an interview, came from an agency called Robert Sharp and Partners. It was a small agency where my then girl friend Caroline worked. At that time she happened to be on holiday in France. Throughout the previous summer Caroline had regaled me with wondrous tales of the exciting and glamorous life at Robert Sharps. The agency was owned and run, she had told me, by three handsome, clever, charming, witty young Old Etonians. They were called Oliver Knox, Mark Ramage, and Christopher Murray. All ex-scholars at Kings, all Firsts, all things bright and beautiful. (I learned later that in her enthusiasm Caroline had over-romanticized some of the facts a little, though most were accurate enough.) Caroline working at Robert Sharps meant that I could not. I had heard all manner of frightening stories describing the dreadful consequences of dirtying one's own doorstep. But as Caroline was away on holiday, I went along to the interview for the ride.

Not wanting the job I had a few drinks beforehand. I strolled into the interviewing room with the characteristic bravery of a non-combatant and slouched uninvited into one of the armchairs.

'You don't seem particularly nervous, Mr. Fletcher,' one of the glamorous trio remarked.

'I'm not particularly.' I was rather drunk but I neglected to add that.

'Would you like a drink?' another of them asked. He was wearing a bow tie and red felt braces. All three were jacket-less, one with his shirt open-necked. Not at all the stern, formal interviewers' uniform that I had met previously; clearly a foxy ploy, the purpose of which I could not fathom.

'Yes please. Sherry.'

'I see,' said one of them studying my letter of application, 'that you worked as a ladies' shoe salesman during one of your long vacations.'

'Yes.'

'What did you learn from that?'

'That not many women wash their feet before they go to buy shoes.' My weak facetiousness won no smile.

'Is that all?'

I paused and wrinkled my brow in an effort of mock concentration. 'Corns and bunions are far more common among the female population than I'd have guessed.'

'Didn't you learn anything about the techniques of selling?'

'Not much. I only did the job for three weeks. Then I was fired.'

'Why?'

'I suppose I wasn't very good at selling shoes to ladies with bunions and dirty feet.'

My interrogator appeared to decide that he had exhausted that line of enquiry, and changed the subject. 'Now that you've met us, what do you think you would most dislike about working here?'

Again I was nonplussed. Surely, by the Authorised Rules of the Game, he was supposed to ask that question the other way around, in the positive? I eyed him cautiously, like a poker player searching his opponent's face for the tell-tale twinge of a double-bluff. 'Are you particularly unpleasant people to work with?' I scored a grin.

'Do you know anything about working in advertising?'

I recalled that in my letter to the Box Number I had omitted to mention that I was already working at Mather and Crowther. Changing jobs so quickly might have suggested to a prospective employer a less than perfectly stable personality.

'I've had a few interviews with other agencies.'

'Which?'

'Um ... Mather and Crowther, London Press Exchange, S.H. Benson...'

'Who did you meet at your Mather and Crowther interviews?'

'Um ... Stanhope Shelton.' I felt myself slipping into an awkward situation.

'What did you make of him?'

Only one of the three of them seemed to be asking questions.

I guessed he was Oliver Knox, whom Caroline had told me was the chattiest and wore bow ties. The other two seemed unaware of my presence. Ramage or Murray was doodling, Murray or Ramage was thoughtfully picking his nose. Were these calculatedly sinister interview techniques intended to intimidate me?

'Shelton asked far sharper questions than you're doing.'

For the first time Ramage and Murray showed signs of mild interest. 'Such as?'

I had slipped a little further. 'Such as was it just because of the money that I want to get into advertising?'

'Is it?' asked Murray or Ramage.

'Not entirely.'

'That's always seemed to me a frightfully dull question.' Knox returned to the fray. 'Tell me, what impressions did you gain of Stanhope Shelton? Describe his character in, say, fifty words.'

Having slid into the mire, the situation was now past saving. I had been a trainee copywriter at Mather and Crowther for four weeks, had met Shelton several times and had gossiped about him endlessly in the pubs at lunchtimes.

'Well, just on the basis of one interview he seems ... very volatile, a bit hasty. Sharp rather than intelligent, I'd say, but very perceptive of social minutiae ... prides himself on being forthright.'

'You seem to have interviewed your interviewer rather effectively,' Murray or Ramage said.

'One does try to.' I was feeling both a little drunker and a little bolder.

'What do you make of the three of us?' Knox asked, beginning to giggle. 'Would you like another drink?'

The interview was obviously going well. Pity about not being able to take the job.

'Yes please.' I stared at them all, thinking as hard as my befuddled brain would allow. Presumably they thought I was summing them up. I was trying to remember everything Caroline had said about them, and to edit it into an expurgated version which would not make my knowledge obvious. 'Well,' I said looking at Knox's red braces, 'you're not exactly working-class lads on the way up. Good minor public school I'd guess,' hoping that might wound their Etonian pride, 'perhaps Clifton or Oundle. Very sure of yourselves—though I must say I can't see why. Probably quite intelligent ... for people in advertising, I mean ... and rather snobbish too....'

The interview meandered to an end amid gales of happy but no doubt shrewdly analytical laughter. They offered me the job the next day, and as Caroline left both me and them shortly afterwards, I handed in my notice at Mather and Crowther after two months and started in advertising for the second time.

Very few people have the particular talents necessary to be really good at making advertising. Perhaps a hundred in Britain. In some ways the problems of finding and recruiting them are very similar to those of the Civil Service. In the Civil Service too, as in the professions, there are no stocks, no capital, the inventory lives by its wits and goes home every night; and there are no formal qualifications for entry. To cope with the problem the Civil Service has constructed an elaborate system of examinations and tests, far more sophisticated than anything we snakily-scheming admen have devised, for entrants seeking admission at the higher levels. It was this analogy that prompted Oliver Knox to run his Most Unusual Seminar.

In 1962 all the leading undergraduate newspapers and magazines in the country carried a large, dignified advertisement. It read:

A MOST UNUSUAL SEMINAR

> Robert Sharps, the most brilliant of all the advertising agencies, are looking for the most brilliant of this year's graduates. They propose to invite up to twenty of you, after a long interrogation in London, to spend a weekend with them during this Easter vacation. The hospitality at this weekend will be almost vulgarly profuse. Continual distractions will be offered. But there will also be one written paper of the most taxing kind. It will need great stamina to endure it all. Any man, or girl who does survive will immediately be offered a glittering job at £1,000 a year.

The response was overwhelming. Applications poured in by the hundred. One of Oliver Knox's original hypotheses, that an irreverent approach would attract many intelligent undergraduates who otherwise would not dream of entering advertising, still less of applying to Robert Sharps, was fully vindicated. Whittling the applications down to a short list took weeks.

Eventually the chosen short list attended the promised seminar. We threw a special cocktail party for them; they stayed at the Ritz, and ate at expensive restaurants. They also took a long written paper, were interviewed and grilled continuously, and played a difficult computer business game. As a selection procedure the operation was a complete success. Except for the publicity. A journalist from the *Sunday Telegraph* attended the seminar. Predictably she published a sensationalist piece headlined A FIRM PICKS ITS NEW EXECUTIVES AT A VULGAR WEEKEND. The article was replete with journalistic descriptions of the lavish entertainment, less full of information about the more serious aspects of the seminar. It did Sharps a lot of harm. Lest they had missed it the head of another advertising agency spitefully sent copies of the article to all our clients, with a covering letter enquiring whether they realized that they were associated with an agency which interviewed young men by getting them drunk at cocktail parties—as if barristers had never invented dinners.

Why does one want to work in advertising? Everyone working in an agency has his own private and confidential answer. I like it because I work with many different companies in many different industries. This gives a broader view of business than working in one or two companies possibly could. I like it because it is a tense, nervy, fast-moving, manic-depressive business in which one almost never has the time to be bored. Yossarian would hate it. I like it because there are more intelligent, quirky, flamboyant people in advertising than in most other lines of business. I like it because I believe advertising to be a necessary, worthwhile and productive occupation. Lastly, with Stanhope Shelton I like advertising because you can earn a fairly high salary fairly quickly. If you are good you should easily be earning £2,500 a year by the age of twenty-five and £5,000 a year by the age of thirty. 'I sold my interest in Benton and Bowles when I was thirty-five,' said former Senator William Benton, 'and I'd been taking three or four hundred thousand dollars a year out of it. Any business where a kid can make that kind of money is no business for old men.'*

What do I dislike about working in advertising? Being attacked continually by intelligent non businessmen who believe advertising to be a worthless, wasteful, philistine business. I dislike many worthless, wasteful, philistine ads that I see, and illogically feel a despairing partial responsibility for them. I dislike advertising personally because it is fundamentally a consultancy, an advisory business; the money you

---

* Quoted by Martin Mayer in *Madison Avenue, USA*, Penguin Books, 1961.

spend is your clients' and they finally call the tune. Lastly, I dislike advertising because it is not a good way to make a lot of money: nobody has ever made a major fortune out of it.*

The devious advertising tycoons, the faceless, power-hungry hidden-persuaders are still asking the same predictable old questions, and any of these answers should do.

----

* John Gunther, in his biography of Albert Lasker, the almost legendary builder of Lord and Thomas Inc., now Foote, Cone and Belding, records that Lasker made $11,500,000 out of advertising—'more than anyone else ever will'. Hardly a pittance, but had Lasker not sold off acres of Texas that he inherited from his father, because he was suspicious of real estate as an investment, that land alone would have been worth $500,000,000—almost fifty times what he made from a lifetime in advertising. (*Taken at the Flood*, Hamish Hamilton, 1960.)

3   Build Your Career on Failure

Having survived the sly selection procedures, the apprentice starts on his initiation and training rites. At Mather and Crowther these comprised a Grand Tour of the agency's departments, sitting quietly in executives' offices, unwelcome and largely ignored. At Robert Sharps, then a less conventional agency, they employed the devastatingly ingenious *Throw-Him-in-at-the-Deep-End-and-See-if-He-Swims Training Plan.*

Two weeks after joining Robert Sharps I found myself working on the Player's Cigarettes and Tobacco account, which the agency had recently won. It is a very important account, of course—a big spender, a prestigious name. I was assisting a director called Norman Griffiths who himself had joined Robert Sharps only a couple of months before. He had never previously worked in an advertising agency and as he was anyway on an extended holiday for most of that summer, I was very much left to my own devices.

My own devices mainly comprised drinking beer for three hours each lunch time with old college friends, all of whom were working equally hard, conscientiously clawing their way up the executive ladder; and reading the *New Yorker* which I had happily discovered came Free and Without Obligation to anyone working in an ad agency. A perk that none of my friends could match.

Sitting at my folding card table—I had no desk—and chuckling over Thurber or Perelman one befuddled afternoon, my telephone rang.

'Player's copy?' said a gruff voice.

'You want the copy department,' I answered brightly. 'I'll transfer you. Who's speaking?'

'*Reader's Digest*. Copy for November issue. Whole page, Player's Tobacco. Need a plate tomorrow.'

'A plate?'

'You're not expecting us to set are you?'

I could tell from his tone of voice that it would be unwise to ask him to set. 'No ... no ... what do you want a plate for?'

'Can't go beyond midday tomorrow. That's the deadline.'

'But you were talking about the November issue? It's only August.'

'A plate tomorrow. And no extensions.'

The conversation had been mysterious, but I sensed that it called for action on my part. Perhaps if I returned to the Small and Serene Night Life of Manhattan it might all go away. Perhaps not.

Norman Griffiths was on holiday, and the other directors of the agency were out. Finally I found the production manager and inquired why *Reader's Digest* should need a plate the next day for their November issue.

'Have you got the artwork?'

'Artwork? I think it's going to be a photograph. Anyway I haven't got anything.'

'No artwork? We'll never get a plate by tomorrow then. That's trouble. Missing our first copy date on Player's.'

'Oh.'

'Let's talk to the art director.'

The art director was not in a helpful mood. 'I've not got any bloody artwork,' she fumed angrily. 'Nobody told me it was bloodywell needed today. The photographs have only come in this minute. I've not looked at them yet.'

'The man from *Reader's Digest*,' I said firmly, 'is not expecting to set.'

The production manager and art director, normally at war with each other, for that moment forgot their differences and together glared at me in mute hostility. The enthusiastically incompetent graduate trainee is never warmly welcomed by the experience hardened workers. From the moment he steps jauntily into the company, they know that he will leave a trail of chaos and confusion which inevitably they will have to clear up.

'How long,' the production manager asked the art director, 'will it take to get artwork?'

'God knows. Can't we delay the insertion?'

'Too late now. I can lay on overnight work at the plate-makers. If we get artwork to them by three in the morning we'd get a plate to the *Digest* by midday tomorrow.'

The art director looked around for something heavy to throw, but could find nothing suitable close to hand. 'I'm not bloodywell working all night again. No. No. No,' she screamed. 'Just because he's screwed it all up again. That's final. Get someone else to bloodywell do it. I've had enough.' She climbed down from her high stool and pushing past me violently slammed the door. The bang would certainly have woken anyone in the building lucky enough still to be enjoying a post-lunch nap.

'Oh dear.' I was left in her office with the production manager.

'Don't worry, she'll do it. She'll be back in a minute.'

She was and she did.

They worked all night, while I stood around drinking the agency's gin to keep their morale high. At eleven o'clock I went to a photographer's to collect the pack shot which had been taken that evening. Returning at midnight I found myself locked out. There was no bell. I shouted up at the tall modern building; no one heard. I tried to climb up to an accessible open window but was restrained by a policeman who believed not a word of my story and threatened to arrest me for attempted burglary. In the half light, and somewhat distraught, I suddenly feared that I might be suffering a hallucination.

'Aren't you Georgie Wise?' I asked timidly.

'Aren't you Winston Fletcher?'

Our noisy laughter echoed in the quiet empty street.

'When did you become a cop?'

'About four years ago. What've you been doing since you left school?'

Georgie and I, though never close friends, had suffered

maths and Latin together for six years in the same form
It was an incredible coincidence, but his timely arrival was
clearly the act of some divine agent who was disposed towards me kindly.

'Been to Cambridge. Now I work in this advertising agency.
Here, give me a leg up to that window.'

Georgie ruminated on the problem for a moment. 'Fraid
not, Winston. Unless you can prove to me you are the bona
fide owner of the building, your entry through that window
would constitute unlawful breaking and entering.'

'Oh rubbish, Georgie. I've explained the mess I'm in.'

'Sorry, old chum. It's me job. Can't help you.'

We had never been close friends. I could distinctly remember having had a punch-up with him when he had scrawled
four-letter words on one of my exercise books. Surely he had
not been bearing a grudge for nearly a decade?'

'But Georgie this is ridiculous...'

'No go. That's it.' He interrupted me, marched resolutely
across the street and stood stiffly to attention, staring warn-
ingly at me and at the open window.

I was dumbfounded, but my pride forbade me to argue
with him further. Mumbling violent oaths to myself, con-
demning Georgie, his ancestors and his offspring to eternal
violent indignities, I slunk off down the road, away from the
beleaguered building. I went to a telephone booth and rang
every line, but nobody replied. There they were in the building, waiting for me to come back with the photograph and
cursing me yet again for my ineptitude. I had wasted over
an hour trying unsuccessfully to get in. There was only one
solution. To go to one of the directors' homes and get a key.
I woke up the managing director, Mark Ramage, at about
two o'clock. It's one way of establishing that you're working
late.

Professor Thomas Berg of New York University has published a lovely book called *Mismarketing**. It is a collection
of beautiful business bungles, assembled and documented

---

* *Mismarketing : Case Histories of Marketing Misfires* by Thomas L.
Berg. Published Nelson, 1971.

with loving care. General Foods, Esso, Du Pont, Ford and other mighty names skid across his pages on banana skins, and fall flat on their corporate bums. He quotes:

> There must be attitudes of calculated risk-taking, of willingness to make a few mistakes for the sake of many successes. The only way to avoid mistakes is never to do anything new or different, to create, to grow. The winner is the Company that is willing to make mistakes —but organizes to keep them fewer and less severe than those of competitors.

Which sounds fine in theory. It's what we all learn in Grade I Infants Business School. Unfortunately it was not the consciously taken deliberate business risks with which my early days in advertising were crowded. It was unconscious, accidental bloomers.

Despite the fiasco of the *Reader's Digest* tobacco ad, Player's entrusted us with the launch of Admiral, a new king-size cigarette. At that time, in 1959, the king-size market was growing rapidly: 'exploding' was the adjective frequently used in the business press. In the previous few months Churchman's had launched Churchman's 'K', Wills had launched Kingsway, both king-size brands—and neither had been successful. Nevertheless, experience from everywhere else in the world proved that the trend was to king-size. It was clearly urgent for Player's to get in with their entry. We spent about £200,000 in two months on television and in the Press, and maybe sold a couple of packs. We then spent almost £100,000 in four weeks in the London area and achieved sales of an asterisk on a Nielsen chart.

There was a fine post mortem. It turned out the pack colour was wrong. We had market-researched packs of a slightly different colour to the ones that were finally launched, because the few packs needed for the research had been printed silk-screen whereas the mass-production packs could not be. The cigarette was wrong. Believing the king-size market still to be exploding, we had taste-tested the cigarette among smokers generally; king-size smokers are a particular minority and they wanted a much milder flavour. The advertising was wrong. It too was based on the hypothesis that more and more smokers were switching to king-size every day. Smokers had irritatingly stopped switching a few months previously. The name Admiral was wrong. The great naval cigarette tradition was anathema to the young dollies who smoke king-size. The whole product idea was one great big wonderful mistake.

I was learning about the rough and tumble of business life. A few days before the launch it occurred to me lying in bed one night that something was awry. I got up and wrote a document showing that the king-size market had lost its fizz, and recommended an immediate stop to all activity.

'How long,' Norman Griffiths asked the next morning after reading quickly through it, 'have you now been in advertising?'

'Seven months,' I replied proudly, waiting to be congratulated on having shown great perspicacity for one so inexperienced.

'If,' he said, 'you expect this whole launch to be called off at the eleventh hour because of the naïve views of a neophyte still wet behind the ears, you have a lot to learn. Take this nonsense away,' he handed me my carefully composed report, 'and don't let me hear another word about it.'

In 1959 the great post-war boom in unit trust sales began. The launch of Save and Prosper Group's Income Unit Trust was dedicated to the widely held view that the mass market for unit trusts was at hand. Once again I was lucky enough to be in on an exploding market. Market research had shown that the cloth-cap worker—the vogue phrase at the time— liked the idea of unit trusts when exposed to it and was ready willing and able to buy Income Units. The Save and Prosper Group budgeted £90,000 for the launch, and the money all had to be spent in a weekend. It's quite difficult to spend £90,000 in a weekend.

We used television, the popular Press, women's magazines and almost every local morning paper we could find. The Friday evening before the papers were due to carry the first announcement advertisements I suddenly realized that all the Sunday ads included a terrible howler. 'Go to your bank TODAY,' they stated boldly, 'and invest in Income Units NOW.'

Oh God! Proofs of the advertisements had been seen and studied carefully at the agency and by innumerable people at the Save and Prosper Group. They had been signed as approved by copy-writers and art directors, by solicitors and accountants, and investment managers. It was everyone's fault, but that was irrelevant. I had a vision of millions of cloth-cap workers battering at their bank doors on Sunday morning, desperate to buy their Income Units. I had a vision of myself being fired on Monday.

On the Saturday morning I telephoned every Sunday news-paper in the country and begged them to change the ad-vertisements—which they are rightly very reluctant to do once a proof has been approved. The advertisement appeared with 'Today' and 'Now' corrected to 'Tomorrow' by each paper in a host of different typefaces. Nobody noticed. Only the Hebrides edition of the *News of the World*, which had gone to press on the Friday, carried the error. If there was a bank manager on the Hebrides embarrassed that Sunday, I hope that he will now accept my belated apologies.

I need not have bothered. The cloth-cap workers did not flock to buy Income Units. The launch was a flop and the Save and Prosper Group lost about £60,000.

These two launches taught me to be exceedingly wary of exploding markets. Men's toiletries and partwork publications, packaged holidays and bath additives, menthol cigarettes and biological washing powders, vaginal deodorants and table wines and instant mashed potatoes—each of these and many others have been fashionable growth markets. Manufacturers have chased each other into them like lemmings. Only to lose a small fortune.

The prerequisites for a dangerously exploding market are three:

Firstly, conventional wisdom says that *in the long run,* for underlying sociological or economic reasons (usually to do with the affluent society or some other serious-sounding cliché) the particular market is *bound* to grow.

But growth can be a long time coming and precocity can be expensive.

Secondly, articles appear in the business and trade Press publicizing the explosion.

As a rule of thumb, in business it is safe to assume that by the time the Press knows about something everybody involved has known about it for months, if not years.

Thirdly, the product field is one where the manufacturing process is comparatively simple—so that product differences are thought to be largely marketing and image differences.

Which is true of far fewer markets than either marketing men or the public believe; and when it is true, finding real and acceptable image differences is at least as difficult as developing product advantages.

Markets explode quite easily. Word goes round that sales of a particular product are booming. Everyone hurries to get in quick for fear of being too late. And that's the way the bubble bursts.

The amazing thing, with all the clangers and errata which occur in business every day, is that the public continues to think of advertising men as all-powerful Machiavellian manipulators; instead of realizing that it's still largely a matter of unscientific hunch and judgement. The ad makers are seen as cunning power-game schemers whose every plot comes out as planned. It's a myth to which we who are in the business like to subscribe, of course. Much nicer to think of ourselves as Masters of our Destiny than as Hostages to Fortune.

It is commonplace that young men are almost invariably over-eager, blindly optimistic and dangerously enthusiastic about projects in which they get involved. Every apprentice brand manager, copywriter or account executive rushes to get a success under his belt, a triumph for his curriculum vitae. In practice, most businessmen who end up as successes seem to start their careers by displaying an almost phenomenal facility for failure. The late Douglas Collins—founder of Goya, builder of Suttons Seeds, self-made millionaire and entrepreneur extraordinary—included in his entry in *Who's Who*: '...started unsuccessful businesses, 1933-36...'

I believe the explanation is that you can learn a great deal more from failures than from successes. But beware of simple explanations of causality. While successes tend to be very specific, failures are more general. The many facets of a marketing mix that go to make up a success cannot usually be separated and transposed to other situations. (Though one often hears marketing men trying: 'We used television very successfully for Burpo so I'm sure it will be right for Bilge.') Whereas things that have gone wrong once will almost invariably go wrong again. And in really big, high-quality smasheroo disasters every aspect of the mix will probably have contributed its own little bit.

So I suppose that during my freshman year in advertising I was extraordinarily lucky. Everything I touched turned to dust. Every campaign I worked on ended in catastrophe, every decision brought disaster. It was a long series of miserable blessings in disguise. We all have our ups and downs, so that after so many downs I was owed a good few ups. The only thing to fear about failure is to be frightened of admitting to it. Sufficient blunders will make even the most optimistic young tyro pause for mental refreshment.

Inquests concentrate the mind wonderfully.

4 The Client/Agency Relationship

I started in advertising as a trainee copywriter. My fourth day on the Agency Grand Tour I ate my first expense-account lunch. Stilton, French bread, and Beaujolais in Henekey's in the Strand. I was with the account executive on Sanatogen Tonic Food and his client the advertising manager. That morning, prior to my free lunch, I had sat through an excruciatingly tedious meeting during which the client had briefed the account executive on the next year's Sanatogen campaign. Sanatogen has been the same successful product since the dawn of time, and there was clearly no real need for a new campaign—except as evidence of industry, to prove that ad manager and ad agency alike were hard at it, earning their keep. Hence the client's brief was of the vaguest possible kind, punctuated liberally with such pellucid phrases as 'you-know-what-I-mean' and 'you-know-the-sort-of-thing-I'm-getting-at'. To inspire extra enthusiasm in the agency, the client waved his arms in the air a good deal.

I was aware, even after three-and-a-half days, that it would eventually be my task, the copywriter's task, to interpret precisely what the client's woolly words meant. It would one day be my job to create hard-selling advertisements from that jelly-soft brief. I began to feel that perhaps my meagre creative talent had bitten off more than it could chew.

At lunch, over the Stilton, the nasty little advertising problems were quickly forgotten. The account executive regaled us with one dirty joke after another. His repertoire was jumbo-size. We laughed and laughed. I started to tell a few jokes myself. I quite fancied myself as a dab hand with a blue joke in those days. The client laughed. The account executive laughed. I decided that I rather liked free Stilton, French bread and Beaujolais. I decided that I was likely to be far more successful in advertising as an entertainer than as a copywriter. I decided to switch from being a trainee copywriter to being a trainee account executive. The very title sounded superior.

Over the years many ad agencies have tried to dispense with account executives. There is a good, creative agency in London called Lippa, Newton working to this theory right now. Their argument seems irrefutable: account executives carry messages backwards and forwards between client and agency. Bad account executives get the messages wrong and are a disaster. Good account executives are rare and extremely expensive. Creative people get deeper into advertising problems and do better work when they are directly briefed by clients; clients prefer personally to brief the people who do the work rather than deal with middlemen who are bound occasionally to garble their messages. For the price of a good account executive an agency can afford an extra good writer. Account executives are nugatory parasites living off the produce of the workers, superfluous excrescences getting in the way of good ads. Provided the agency has an efficient internal traffic and co-ordination system, who needs them?

The account executive is indeed a glorified messenger boy. This is not as disparaging as it may sound. It is exceptionally difficult to receive and transmit complex messages accurately as anyone who has played Pass-The-Whisper knows. The simplest message passed along a chain of four or five people will be distorted beyond recognition. Moreover many of the messages that an account executive must carry cannot be put concisely into words. If they could, the dictum that 'verbal instructions should never be given or accepted; all instructions must be confirmed in writing' would dissolve away all the difficulties. Very few businessmen are incisive and articulate. Sadly my Sanatogen meeting was anything but atypical.

Take the common or garden meeting when the account executive, with a suitable preamble and fanfare of trumpets, presents an ad which the client promptly rejects. All too often the client can say only that the ad is not quite right, but he cannot precisely say why; he senses something is wrong, but cannot put his finger on just what. His objections cannot be discounted merely because they have not been clearly verbalized. All of us frequently see a tie or a dress which we like but decide against buying because we 'feel it would not suit us'—without being able to define exactly why.* Obviously coherent, pithy instructions and comments are preferable to incoherent grunts. But, *pace* Wittgenstein's *Tractatus*, whereof one's clients cannot speak, thereof the account executive cannot remain silent. He must merely convince himself that his client has a legitimate and significant point; he must be certain that the client has not merely reacted to the ad thoughtlessly.

After lengthy debate, the account executive will realize the client is adamant and he will have gleaned as much as he can as to what is wrong. He tries to unravel the new, turbid brief on the way back to the agency. To report to the writer and artist who may (or admittedly, may not) have slaved for weeks on the rejected ad: 'The client didn't like it but he couldn't say why,' will infuriate them. To invent phoney but logical criticisms which the client *might* have raised will inevitably mean eventual chaos. Somehow the poor account executive must translate his client's vague emotions into specific instructions. These instructions will evoke the spirit of the client's view in such a way that the correct actions can be taken: if the new ad is wrong again, the client will not be amused. The way of the glorified messenger boy is no primrose path.

I had a client who had been a sergeant-major until some quirk of management lateral thinking transmuted him into an advertising manager. His way of getting the best out of the agency was to telephone every morning at 0931 and give me my orders for the day. At the same time he would reprimand me for my misdemeanours of the day before.

---

* There are of course distinguished antecedents for all this. Albert Einstein, referring to the genesis of his ideas on Relativity said, 'These thoughts did not come in any verbal formulation. I rarely think in words at all.'

'Fletcher,' his voice would bark through my early morning somnolence, 'Fletcher! We briefed you at 1100 hours the day before yesterday. When are we going to see your proofs?' (He meant roughs.)

'Fletcher, there's another spelling mistake in this copy. You've spelt "it's" "its". No. Perhaps you're right. It's it is. Correction withdrawn.'

'Fletcher, where are those bloody media schedules? Asked your secretary for them ten days ago. Beginning to think there's some funny business between you and her, you know. Should have been fired months ago. Lazy bitch.'

I grew terrified of each morning's alarm call. Sometimes I deliberately arrived late, hoping that having missed me at 0931 hours he might forget to try again. No such luck. 'Late again, Fletcher. Have a word with Ramage, you know. Not used to service like this.'

I wept on every shoulder I could find, and Oliver Knox determined that he would revenge me. He joined a meeting I was in one morning. 'How,' he asked angelically, 'do you think a client would get the best from his agency?' The client replied. Oliver continued his sardonic interrogation on my behalf. 'And would you think an intelligent client would shout at its agency and bully it?'

The client became extremely irritable under the continuing inquisition.

'Then,' said Knox, administering the *coup de grâce*, 'why do you behave in such an appallingly uncivilized way to poor Winston here? It does not do you nor your company nor us any good.'

Unfortunately Knox had chosen the wrong meeting and the wrong client for his well-intentioned support of his troops.

Nobody in an agency suffers so deeply when an account is lost as the account executive. The service departments, working on many other accounts, can absolve themselves from personal responsibility for the loss. The directors quickly immerse themselves in replanning the long-term future of the agency, studying designs for the new décor in the lavatories and deciding other vital matters of moment. The account executive knows that his career has been stunted, even if only temporarily; he knows that everyone in the agency blames him, while they politely listen to and ignore his excuses and explanations. Worst of all, he suddenly realizes that his client, the erstwhile friend with whom he has shared so many lunches at the Terrazza and whiskies in the Salisbury, has punched him on the nose and kicked him in the crutch—no doubt apologizing the while. To be kept cheerful and full of fun, account executives need constant care and attention. Here are seven nice, reassuring remarks with which kind clients can keep their account executives happy:

> Thanks awfully for getting me out of that hole.
> Hasn't your secretary got super legs? (rhetorical)
> Would you like me to write to your boss saying something nice about you?
> You're the best account exec I've ever worked with. (This comes better from an older man.)
> You and I are just like two peas in a pod; and/or you and I are just like sausages out of the same sausage machine.
> You know you're just like me, a little shy.
> In the end, you know, client-agency relationships are nothing more than just chemistry.

And here are seven nasty, unsettling remarks with which unkind clients can bring their account executives to the brink of nervous trauma:

> Could you let me have a detailed breakdown and explanation of these production invoices, old boy? (not at all rhetorical)
> Why can't I ever get through to your switchboard?
> I don't think much of your new secretary.
> You never seem to be in your office these days.
> I do like creative/media/production/traffic/teaboys to attend meetings whenever possible.
> I suppose you also work on much bigger accounts than ours.

In the end I suppose client/agency relationships are nothing more than just chemistry.

Account executives are at the very heart of the ad agency business. When a client appoints an agency, he is not looking only for excellent creative work or only for cost-efficient media buying. Those services are vital, but they can be obtained from specialists outside of agencies. Agencies exist to plan total campaigns: the creative content must be interwoven with the media plan and with below-the-line promotions. The agency needs to understand and be involved in advertisement pre-tests, marketing analyses, new product strategy and old product improvement. As all the textbooks say, it is the job of the account executive to co-ordinate this diversity of work, and to communicate progress and setbacks on all fronts to the client. He is a jack of all trades and master of none, which inevitably means that he will irritate most of the specialists and experts whom it is his job to guide. Above all therefore, the account executive must be a lovable diplomat. Few people can be more irritating than lovable diplomats.

One of the clients I have most liked was Paul Hocking Baker. Paul was deputy chairman of IPC Magazines Ltd., for whom our agency was then launching a series of part-work publications. That year IPC Magazines Ltd. were our largest clients. Paul took my wife and I to see Sadlers Wells' *Ariadne auf Naxos* at the Coliseum. We sat in a box. It is a pity neither my wife nor I appreciate opera, because I am told it was rather a good production. After *Ariadne* we dined at the Savoy. Paul ate at the Savoy quite often and was an honoured customer.

'Good evening, Mr. Hocking Baker. Good evening, Mr. Hocking Baker,' the waiters chanted as we were led to the finest table in the restaurant, close to the stage. The service was flawless, drinks appeared and disappeared as if by magic, the food was delicious and I slowly recovered from the opera, aided by several large glasses of fine claret and a grouse.

P.H.B. was an excellent and generous host. At 11.30 the lights dimmed, the stage beside us levitated, and the cabaret began.

'My lords, ladies and gentlemen,' a disembodied voice boomed over the loudspeaker system, 'tonight the Savoy is very proud to present to you, from France, that internationally famous star of stage, screen and radio, my lords, ladies and gentlemen ...'

'Who?' I whispered to my companions.

'Never heard of her.'

The Savoy band struck up her opening song, and out on to the apron promontory strode—there is no other word for it—a statuesque lady of Amazonian proportions singing Chevalier songs in an accent that I would have sworn emanated from the environs of Petticoat Lane rather than of Paris, but for the fact that I knew for certain that the Savoy would never fib about such things. After a few songs she paused, and descended the stairs towards her audience, whispering huskily into the microphone as she did so. 'And now, ladies and gentlemen, I am going to select a gentleman from une table ce soir to come on to ze stage wiz me and dance ... a tango. Ladies and gentlemen 'oo shall be ze lucky man 'oo will dance wiz me tonight?'

Horror of horrors, she was sitting on my lap. As may have been gathered, I found her particularly unappealing. I am no shy mouse, but at that moment I would far sooner have been trying to hold a polite cocktail-party conversation with a cobra or removing a nest of daddy-long-legs from my bath. I should have been pleasurably basking in the aftermath of an especially gorgeous meal. Instead I was being mauled by a lady, sitting without invitation on my knee, who was going to press me into publicly tangoing with her on stage.

'My darlink,' she ruffled my hair and the audience roared. 'My darlink, do you weesh to dance ze tango wiz me?' With each word she breathed heavily into the microphone as if she was rapidly approaching a sexual climax. She was no mean performer.

'No.'

'But, my darlink, why not? Are you afrraid perrraps of

what weel 'appen when you dance ze tango wiz me?'

'No.'

I estimated there were about two hundred customers in the restaurant, and they had come to watch a jolly cabaret. I wished to spoil neither their evening nor her act. Nor had I the slightest intention of mounting the stage to dance with her. I toyed with the idea of wresting the microphone from her and throwing it—and her too, though I remember doubting if I were strong enough—across the room.

'Are you shy, my darlink?'

'No, I just don't dance.' She held the microphone close to my lips so that every word reverberated loudly.

'But, my darlink, you 'ave such a sexy voice. You *must* come on to ze stage wiz me.'

'No. Honestly.'

The audience catcalled and whistled. I could see her wondering whether to ditch me as a lost cause and go to another table, or whether to persevere with me having invested so much time and effort. Around the room were a score of men who would obviously have been delighted to be the temporary object of her professional affections.

'Tell me, sexy voice, tell me whad is your name?'

The microphone was an inch from my mouth. If Paul Hocking Baker had not been with me I would have lied. Peter or John or David are good names for moments like that. Winston is not. In my earliest schooldays I learned that, despite our great wartime leader, Winston is a joke-name guaranteed to provoke riotous mirth in schoolboys; later in life I learned that it generally has the same effect upon drunks.

'Winston.'

The audience roared with delight. I have never understood why, in certain circumstances, people find the name so funny, but they do.

The *chanteuse* shrewdly saw that Winston was no name for a French lady to mock. 'Winston is not a sexy enough name for you. I shall call you Frou Frou.'

Despite the dead weight on me my reflexes squirmed violently. My subconscious was no doubt desperate to escape from the indignities being perpetrated upon it.

'Now, Frou Frou, I inseest. Come on to ze stage, Frou Frou, and I weel teach you ze tango...' She dropped her already baritone voice another half an octave. 'Frou Frou ... pleeze.'

It was at that moment that I understood, as if by divine revelation, the profound essence of the account executive's existence. Had I been with a friend or a relative or any other kind of business associate I would have thrown the lady off my knee and scarpered. But I knew in my bones that it was my bounden duty to stand by, or rather sit by, my client. To desert a client, and at the Savoy, would be unthinkable.

'Could it be, Frou Frou, that you are embarrassed to dance wiz me for some reason?' Then the Junoesque artiste asked, 'Are you married, Frou Frou?'

Foolishly I failed to see the trap coming. 'Yes.'

'Perraps the lady you are sitting weez is not your wife, eh Frou Frou?'

She wasn't. She was someone else's wife. My own wife was at the far side of the table; but it did not seem to be the right moment to correct her on such a minuscule detail.

'Perraps you don't want to be seen on the stage because ze lady is not your wife, eh Frou Frou? Is she your wife Frou Frou?'

'Who?'

'Zees lady 'ere you are sitting wiz.'

'No.'

In the traditional jargon of her profession, that brought the roof down. The cheers were thunderous, the table-thumping tumultuous, the yells appalling. At last she seemed satisfied and having brought that particular part of her act to a satisfactory finale, she decamped.

The client/agency relationship is quite unique, a miasma of inferences and shadows. The liaison has four particular facets. Agencies tend to have only a few large customers, each of which is likely to account for between five per cent and twenty per cent of its turnover and profits. Most other businesses, and certainly most professional businesses, have a very large number of small customers. This is one reason why agencies get so feverishly excited about gaining or losing clients. A second reason is that clients tend to stay with agencies for many years. Other companies which trade with only a few large customers can usually complete their deals and move on. Agencies expect and pray that their clients will stay with them unto eternity. Thinking that far ahead involves intense mental strain.

Another curiosity of the advertising agency industry is that there is no price competition. So that competition between agencies takes vaguer, more subtle forms. Finally, the product the agency sells its clients is a will-o'-the-wisp, insubstantial and largely immeasurable.

There was a vogue about ten years ago for clients to set their agencies defined targets and objectives*—as if they were Marks and Spencer specifying the quality of a cotton vest. Certain aspects of advertising, particularly television-time buying, can successfully be subjected to such disciplines. But on a day-to-day basis there are innumerable little jobs to which no objective criteria can be brought, and seat-of-the pants emotional reactions necessarily dictate the decisions.

Individually, none of these situations is unique to the advertising business. Together they interact to produce a curious, tense, almost romantic relationship at the centre of which is the lovable-messenger-boy-diplomat himself.

---

* The influential work on this subject, DAGMAR (*Defining Advertising Goals for Measured Advertising Results*), was published in the USA in 1961. It was a brave attempt at quantifying advertising effectiveness, but it was riddled with logical flaws and chicken-and-egg problems.

5   Call That an Advert?

Advertising is an applied art. The thoughts and efforts of writers and designers are harnessed to create original, imaginative pictures and words that will sell products. No matter how strikingly original the pictures, no matter how wildly original the words, if they fail to persuade people to buy, they fail. The applied arts which advertising most resembles are architecture and book illustration. In each case the imagination of the artist is fettered by the strict disciplines and demands of the art form.

Before an advertisement is produced its objectives are—or should be—defined very clearly; the message to be communicated, the strategy, must be specified precisely and in detail. It is then the copywriters' and art directors' job to transmute these dead, uninspiring objectives into exciting, emotional advertisements; advertisements which communicate the specified message clearly and exactly, but with impact and verve. The artist's hands are thus shackled securely, while he is required to create original and relevant work unlike any that has gone before it.

The most difficult demarcation to grasp in advertising is the boundary between form and content. The jargon word for form is strategy: the jargon for content is execution. Endless hours are spent in argument over whether particular aspects of an advertisement are strategy or are execution. Unfortunately form and content cannot be neatly divided. They are inextricably intertwined. Write out the Nazi strategy ('... we'll find a megalomaniac midget with a funny moustache, get him to strut around shouting and carrying an ancient sun symbol and maybe he could become Chancellor...') or the plot of Macbeth ('... then there are these three witches...') and they are nonsense.

Clients and agency managements think in terms of strategy. Writers and designers are easily seduced by their own verbal and visual felicities. Having hit upon a striking slogan or a lovely layout, they forget the original message they are trying to put across. Battle begins. The writers and artists feel that the boorish uncivilized executives have failed to appreciate or even understand their brilliantly original creations; the boorish, uncivilized executives suspect that the writers and artists are self-indulgently seeking to produce witty pretty, sophisticated ads which their witty pretty, sophisticated friends will admire.

Nobody can ever be absolutely certain that an advertisement which is outstandingly striking but is not precisely on strategy may not be more effective than a less outstanding ad which boringly says exactly the right things. Many great advertisements defy logical analysis. They can sometimes be rationalised *after* they have appeared (which is why strategies are so often written long after a campaign has started). David Ogilvy put the eyepatch on to Baron von Wrangel in his Hathaway shirt ad because it *felt* right. Just why the Babycham Bambi or Spillers Flour Grader commercials are so effective is impossible precisely to say. The more original and creative the ad is, the more difficult it will be to justify with logic alone. Whether it is 'on strategy' or 'off strategy' becomes a matter of subjective judgement. And when it comes to advertising everyone in sight is replete with subjective judgements.

'Call that an advert?' a not-altogether-refined client once shouted at me, 'call that an advert? I could do better with my knob and a pot of paint.' A difficult point to refute. He was an extremely successful businessman whose name is a household word; he had made many millions of pounds during the war and for all I knew had an exceptionally versatile weapon.

On another occasion he turned upside down all the ads being presented to him. 'A lot of people read ads in other people's papers. In the tube. Don't suppose you Mayfair arties ever go in the tube. Any good advert can be read upside down. And this lot can't.' Not one of the tests which text-

books on advertising mention. But not without merit. I later
sold a campaign to a client by inverting all the ads and
repeating the dictum. That particular campaign looked
rather good upside down.

As a rough generalization, the less important advertising
is to the sales of a product the stronger will be everyone's
feelings about the ads. There is much evidence, for example,
that advertising is of very little, if any, importance in the
success or failure of a cigarette brand. (There is incontro-
vertible evidence that advertising is irrelevant to the total
volume of smoking, as anyone who visits Russia will see;
but that's another matter.) Since advertising is so peripherally
important to the sales of cigarettes, there is no real guidance
as to what constitutes good cigarette advertising. The cigarette companies do lots of ad testing. But such tests are always
of dubious value. As a result everyone in cigarette marketing
can enjoy their subjective opinions unshackled by facts. Everyone does.

When it comes to a market where the ads are crucial to
sales, and particularly where the results can be accurately
measured, you learn to tread more warily. Young copywriters who will happily pontificate about advertisements without brooking contradiction quickly learn the dangers of such
certainty when they are dealing with direct-response advertising, in which each advertisement carries its own coded
coupon and results can therefore be accurately analysed.
Direct-response advertising regularly proves the fallibility of
trying to separate strategy from execution.

A newly appointed guru at the Save and Prosper Group
once asked me to define the creative strategies of the ads then
running. All Save and Prosper's ads carried coupons, and of
course we continuously analysed the results. The most effective ad at the time—indeed the most effective ad I have
ever personally been associated with—was headlined 'How
to Accumulate Lots of Money'. It was written by Oliver
Knox in 1959 and has since run, on and off, for over a decade.
Beyond stating the obvious, that it appealed to naked greed,
I was unable to define its strategy further.

The pedantic guru was not satisfied. He had obviously been reading *Teach Yourself Marketing* or some similar guide on how things should be done. 'There must be,' he said, 'dozens of possible strategies for unit trusts. Go away and write some. And when you've written the strategies, write some damn wonderful ads, just precisely on those strategies.'

A dozen possible strategies were produced. A dozen ads were written, one for each. We tested them all, carefully monitoring the coupon response. 'How to Accumulate Lots of Money' won hands down. Whatever its strategy.

Another successful Save and Prosper ad was headlined 'How to Claim One of Your Most Basic Rights'. This breaks all the theoretical rules. It doesn't mention or give even an inkling of the product being sold. It doesn't appeal to greed particularly, or to fear or to any other simple human emotion. It just happens to be a very interesting headline. And it worked.

Moreover, as important as either strategy or creative interpretation is attention to detail. Not because people read or hear every word or see every facet of an advertisement, but because one ill-chosen word, one false statement or one unbelievable claim can lose the sympathy of some of the audience and therefore reduce the sales effectiveness of the advertisement.

There is an oft-repeated old advertising cliché—quoted by David Ogilvy among others—that the public don't notice typefaces, so long as they are clear and readable. The point is always made ironically, with the aid of a mythical housewife on the top of a Clapham omnibus (or in the Underground) who says to her friend: 'I would have bought that Marmite if only the advertisement headline had not been set in Plantin Bold.'

Because housewives do not mention typefaces does not mean that they are not influenced by them. They are, however minimally. Just as WAR set in 4-inch bold type on the front page of the *Daily Mirror* affects us very differently from 'war' set small and lost in an inside feature. Every single aspect of an ad can be important. One never knows with absolute certainty which aspects will work for you, which against.

Research can help a little. Care and concentrated thought can help much more.

None of which is intended to say that every advertisement's strategy and objectives should not be carefully defined. But content must not dominate form, nor form dominate content. It is a delicate, difficult balance to achieve.

David Ogilvy admits that he is still frequently surprised by which ads do and do not prove to be successful. The more experience you have of advertising, the more humility you learn.

I have been closely involved with approximately 800 campaigns and of course many thousands of individual advertisements. For the great majority of these, perhaps 600, I still have not much idea of whether they were effective or not. Ads are planned, they are written, they appear and they are forgotten. Try to remember last year's ads, let alone those of a decade ago. A very few outstanding ones stick in the memory. Because advertisements are so evanescent their effects can rarely be measured. Nor indeed, outside of coupon-response advertising, are there any perfect means of measurement.

Of approximately 200 campaigns, whose results I can make a sensible, informed guess about, almost as many were ineffective as were effective. This is partly a mathematical phenomenon: once you know a campaign is not working you are bound to change it; once you know a campaign is working you are bound to stay with it. Thus there will always be more unsuccessful campaigns produced than successful ones. But at least I have known some advertisements definitely succeed, others definitely fail. So has every other experienced agency man. I have learnt to tell with my fingertips whether a campaign is likely to work. It takes a long time to learn. That is why grey-beards in agencies get so miffed when a bright young graduate in Unilever delivers a short dissertation on How Advertising Works, while rejecting a campaign on which the agency may have sweated for months.

My own fingertips only react sensitively when I know the complete background to an advertising campaign—know about the product and its advantages over other products, what the public wants from it and everything about it. Which is why advertising awards are so misleading. Every year, in Britain and in the U.S.A. agencies submit their work to panels of jurors who can have no knowledge of what each advertisement is trying to achieve. The jurors do their best. They guess at what the ad's objectives are. Then they guess whether it has succeeded in achieving the objectives they have guessed for it. Inevitably they end up selecting ads which are witty and well designed. Insofar as it is perfectly fair to judge advertisements—or bank notes or vacuum cleaners or wallpaper—as aesthetic objects this is perfectly satisfactory, indeed salutary. It is very desirable that whenever possible, advertisements—and bank notes, vacuum cleaners, wallpaper—should be well designed. Unfortunately, the awards have come to be regarded by many agency creative people, and even by clients, as prizes for *advertising* excellence.

Those who object to advertising awards, and there are many, mock them because the ads that win are often for products which flop. No Domestos or Stork or Fairy Liquid commercial ever wins an award, they say. The function of advertising is to sell products, not to produce graphics. Yet there is no God-given law which says that advertisements which look good *won't* sell products, any more than there is any law which says the opposite.

Occasionally—Volkswagen, Chivas Regal Whisky, Colt Heating are examples—the advertisements which win awards also successfully sell products. This is very misleading. They win awards because the jurors like them. And they happen to advertise products for people who, like the jurors themselves, have degrees in English Literature or went to the Slade.

I have often meant to write an article called 'How the *New Yorker* Ruined British Advertising'. The only American ads to which most UK admen are exposed are in the *New Yorker*, *Esquire* and *Playboy*. The products advertised in those lovely shiny magazines tend to be expensive, sophisticated, and masculine. The ads likewise. A whole school of honest-to-badness advertising has been built up in the *New Yorker*, which mocks the products being advertised. It began, I suspect, with David Ogilvy's classic soft-sell headline: 'At Sixty Miles an Hour the Loudest Noise in the new Rolls-Royce comes from the electric clock'. Ogilvy, in his autobiography, claims this is the best headline he ever wrote. His grounds for this assertion are by no means clear: Rolls's export record in the United States (compared with, say, Mercedes) is hardly a shining one. Whatever the American public's reaction to the deafening electric clock may have been, the advertising industry's reaction was one of total acclaim. The advertisement is included in Julian L. Watkins's *The 100 Greatest Advertisements,** and it spawned the first wave of honest-to-badness advertising.

Following the Rolls-Royce advertisement, Doyle Dane and Bernbach launched a campaign for Volkswagen which, too, has gone down in the annals of advertising history and changed forever the way advertising men think about advertisements. Each VW ad appeared to laugh at the funny little car, to treat it as a joke rather than as the prestige symbol that a car is usually thought to be. One of the greatest of the VW ads was headlined 'Think Small'—sacrilege, traditionalists would have thought, in an American car-advertisement. Volkswagen exports to the US climbed steadily. And— forgetting the quality of the car itself and forgetting the extremely efficient servicing and distribution network that VW had set up nationwide—advertising men came to believe that a little self-deprecation in advertising could actually do no harm. The plagiarists, both in America and here, came on thick and fast. But it's an exceptionally difficult style to emulate.

My favourite inept honest-to-badness campaign was for the launch of the Austin Maxi. 'What's so new about the Austin Maxi?' asked the especially unprovocative headline. And the body copy started: 'Every car advertisement tells you that it has the best engine, gearbox, comfort, roadholding, boot space etc. possible. So maybe the Maxi won't impress you.' The ad then went through each of the Maxi's desirable

---

* *The 100 Greatest Advertisements: Who wrote them and what they did* by Julian Lewis Watkins. Dover Publications, New York, 1959.

qualities somehow managing to make them all sound totally boring. 'What's so new about a new engine? Cars have had them before.' Which must be the plonkest answer to a non-question in the whole history of advertising. 'What's so new about economy gearing? Every car promises better performance at lower cost.' 'What's so new about big boots?' Now, you feel, there must be a joke coming. But no. 'Every car promises an enormous boot.' And finally: 'Will you like the Maxi? We don't have a clue.' Well, one can't say less than that.

When it is done properly, the advertising stratagem in self-denigrating advertising is fairly obvious. Having been candid about something that's wrong with the product, in a forthright let's-all-be-realistic-and-sensible-about-this kind of way, the ad maker hopes that you will believe it when he is being equally honest about what's right with the product. And modesty and humility are so rare in advertising—so the theory goes—that they should be winsome and winning of themselves. Dedicated supporters of the school take the argument still further. They argue that as the level of education steadily increases and as consumers become more sophisticated about the products they buy, they will get progressively more tired of the superlatives and platitudes with which all too many advertisements are stuffed. It is advertising's answer to aggressive consumerism.

For some years honest-to-badness advertisements have been in vogue. To borrow a phrase from Chuck Adams, they have become the new cliché.* A high proportion of each year's advertising awards go to guilt-ridden ads. Many clients rather like them: they minimize the need for the arduous thinking that must go into the finding of a positive sales strategy creatively expressed. They massage the modern educated businessmen's tender conscience about advertising. Sitting in a well-upholstered conference room, surrounded by other marketing men a million miles from Brixton Market, their surface glitter of cleverness and wit are very appealing. Which is fine when one urbane Harvard Business School graduate is

---

* *Common Sense in Advertising* by Charles F. Adams. McGraw Hill, 1965.

communicating with another urbane Harvard Business School graduate via the *New Yorker*'s glossy pages. But sometimes, as in the Maxi ad, one begins to feel that the self-flagellation has turned into simple self-abuse.

There is nothing intrinsically wrong with the honest-to-badness formula. The early VW ads were great. But the approach goes badly awry when it is done gauchely, which it often is; when it is used as a substitute for creative thought, which it often is; and when it is used because its creators feel that in putting on the agony they are also putting on the fashionable style.

Nobody wants to buy imperfect shoddy goods, except at Sale prices. David Ogilvy records—apparently without realizing the significance of the point—that when the chief engineer at the Rolls-Royce factory read the famous advertisement he shook his head sadly and said, 'It's time we did something about that damn clock'. He was right. At £8,000-plus a time, who wants a car with a noisy clock? If I got one I'd complain to the manufacturers.

Honest-to-badness advertising is an extreme genre of advertising devoted to the theory that 'the consumer is a logical, economical, value-analysing being'. In the current consumerist climate it is a fashionable and attractive point of view. It results in the kind of advertising Pierre Martineau* deplored. Martineau rightly believed that human beings' reactions to all products are emotional as well as rational. In an advanced economy where there are rarely any strictly rational reasons for choosing one product rather than another—one chocolate bar or necktie rather than another, Pepsi rather than Coke, Radiant rather than Ariel—such emotional reasons can be all important.

But advertising men and business men, trained in logic and always seeking to justify their decisions in *words* find this situation difficult to cope with. So they analyse and dissect their products, looking for minuscule product advantages which they can put to the consumer—who is not interested. Occasionally admen need to take their creative courage in

---

* *Motivation in Advertising* by Pierre Martineau. McGraw Hill, 1957.

both hands and produce ads which cannot necessarily be logically justified but which, like, emote.

Everyone who writes about advertising invents his own set of Creative Rules. Enjoyable as it would be to promulgate a few new ones, it is a temptation I shall resist. All good advertisements arise out of the product being advertised. And all products are different, no matter how marginally. There can be no formulae. The rules make good rough guidelines, but they are there to be broken. In any case, they relate to details of execution, never to the more fundamental difficulties involved in the development of strategy. Get FREE into the headline if you can. NEW is the most powerful word in the English language and so on. Important stuff, but minutiae.

Rules lead to headaches as often as they lead to solutions. At Mather and Crowther one of Stanhope Shelton's rules was that every headline must include a promise. Sadly the creative group working on Mackeson could discover no promise in their client's stout. It's a pleasant enough beer, and in sufficient quantity it will make you drunk (which, *pace* Kingsley Amis, is no sales claim for any one alcoholic drink because it is well known to be true of all the others). Eventually somebody cracked the problem with an undeniably promissory headline:

There's a promise in a glass of Mackeson.

It conformed to the Shelton's rule, I guess. I never understood it.

Anyone who aspires to produce effective advertising should study the masters: Hopkins, Caples, Bernbach, Ogilvy, Burnett and the rest. Just as a poet or painter would. The way to get better at advertising is to work at it, to study and to work at it some more. Eventually it may come right.

David Abbott—at thirty-two, managing director of Doyle, Dane and Bernbach of London and now a partner in French, Gold, Abbott—is one of the very best copywriters in London. He has been garlanded with awards, and has produced a long string of outstandingly successful campaigns. When he was at Doyle, Dane the chairman of one of his clients, for whom a campaign had just been produced, summoned him. The chairman proceeded to read aloud to him two chapters from *Confessions of an Advertising Man**—'How to Build Great Campaigns' and 'How to write Potent Copy'. David listened silently. At the end of the lesson, the chairman pointed out that none of the ads David had shown him fulfilled Ogilvy's dicta.

If ads could be written by rote, computers could do them quicker. And slicker. At a fraction of the price.

---

* David Ogilvy's famous advertising rulebook. Some of Ogilvy's rules (e.g. always put coupons at the *top* of coupon ads) are totally spurious. Goodness knows how he came by them (Longmans, 1964).

6 Media Muddles

In April 1972 *The Sunday Times* threw a lavish tenth birthday party dinner for its colour *Magazine* at Grosvenor House Hotel. The guest list comprised about 200 advertising people, from clients and agencies, and fifty celebrities—illustrious people who, in the embarrassing words of the invitation, had 'made the decade'.

Just before Peter Cook, perhaps a little overtired, made an unscheduled but impassioned speech complaining bitterly about the scarcity of females present at the gathering, Lord Thomson made his scheduled but less passionate speech of thanks to the advertising industry. Correctly, he thanked advertisers for giving to the world *The Sunday Times Magazine*—a publication created by, for and because of advertisements.

The colour magazines are the archetypal examples of the need of publishers to face both ways: towards their twin masters, sales revenue and advertising revenue. It is a contortionist's trick that some of them cannot do too well, and which has broken some newspapers' necks. It's a trick that Lord Thomson knows all about: hence the party. His selling of *The Sunday Times Magazine* as an advertising medium has been a masterpiece of media marketing. Lord Thomson understands perfectly that despite all the computer analyses and the response curves, despite the many sophisticated mathematical techniques of modern media selection, advertisers buy space in much the same way that housewives buy brands. They try to buy economically, they try to avoid being influenced by the packaging: but finally they frequently buy the products which they happen to like, which they feel warm towards, which they feel to be glamorous, which enhance their self-image.

Lord Thomson knew that his 200 advertising guests at Grosvenor House would be flattered to meet Sir Peter and Lady Medawar, Huw Wheldon, John Braine, Kenneth Tynan, David Jacobs, Jilly Cooper, Alan Sillitoe, Pete and Dud, Jonathan Miller—to mention but a few, and in no particular order. These exalted names were invited so that some of their glamour would rub off on the *Magazine*. Goodness knows why they came. There cannot have been much in it for them, and most of them looked bored to tears. But it was nice for us dull admen to meet them. Hobnobbing with the famous is always good fun. Even when you are perfectly well aware of the game that is being played.

The selection of the most cost-effective media in which to buy advertising space is one of those areas where every intelligent young trainee begins by asking all the right fundamental questions. Discovering that to most of them there are no adequate answers, he soon settles into accepting the prevalent dogma. He quickly comes to feel that since he is busily making decisions which assume the answers to his original basic questions, the questions must have been answered. Just as many of us spend our tortured teens asking 'What is the meaning of life?' and eventually get bored with it when we fail to find a satisfactory answer, so the media planner stops asking 'Are frequent small spaces generally more effective than half-as-frequent spaces twice their size?' as he comes to realize that it is always possible to make a good, sound logical case for each of an almost infinite number of schedules for any campaign.

Prevalent media dogma is based on many myths. These can be divided into three categories*: media 'tactics' myths; media 'medium' myths; and media 'message' myths.

Here are a few media 'tactics' myths:

> Thirty seconds is the most cost/effective length for a television commercial.

---

* Much of this argument is based on D. Richardson's excellent 1971 Thomson Gold Medal Paper: 'Measuring the Role of Media in People's Lives'.

You can't go on television nationally with less than £50,000/£100,000/£150,000/£200,000.

A television rate of strike of less than three peak-time equivalent spots per week is money wasted.

For a new product it is vital to obtain maximum coverage of the prime target audience, even at the expense of frequency.

For a new product it is vital to obtain maximum frequency among the prime target audience, even at the expense of coverage.

And so on. Anyone who has set foot in an advertising agency has heard media directors issue such statements *ex cathedra*, brooking no argument, as if each dictum had somewhere and in some circumstances been proven. They have not. They are based on inconclusive experience, unverifiable intuition and unrigorous logic.

To take one tiny example: there is no sound justification for the rate structure governing the prices of different lengths of television commercial. In the Press it is approximately true that if an advertisement is half the size only half as many people will see it. Therefore advertisers pay for spaces in proportion to their size. This situation does not pertain to television. Nobody argues that half as many people will see a fifteen-second spot as will see the thirty-second spot adjoining it. If, then, the same number of people see it, will only half as many remember it? Who knows? Perhaps it is possible to make twice as strong a sales pitch in twice the length of time? *Twice* as strong? Television rates are determined by the television companies to maximise their revenue. They are manufacturer-orientated rather than market-orientated prices. And media myths have grown up to justify them.

In *The Sunday Times Magazine*'s youth, Lord Thomson threw a birthday party for his lusty infant every year. These parties were a brilliant piece of marketing. Most media regularly entertain agency media specialists—the people directly responsible for buying time and space—and occasionally entertain agency and client management executives. To *The Sunday Times Magazine* birthday parties were invited only agency *creative* staff—more particularly, the people who had written and designed the ads that had appeared in the *Magazine* during the previous twelve months.

At each cocktail party, all of the previous years' ads from the magazine were displayed and the guests voted for the Best Ad of the Year. The champagne flowed freely and a delicious narcissistic time was had by all. *The Sunday Times* made a well-publicized song and dance of only inviting creative people. Any creative man in London who had not succeeded in getting one of his ads, by hook or by crook, into *The Sunday Times Magazine* during the previous year spent a solitary evening, while his habitual pub chums were living it up at The Carlton Tower.

These parties recognized what has since become common knowledge: that media decisions are not the sole prerogative of the agency media specialists. Everyone working on a campaign attends the initial planning meetings, and expresses their views about the media that should be used. The creative people, by nature usually more argumentative, more vociferous and occasionally more articulate than the rest of their colleagues, can be extremely influential in deciding where the ads should appear. At that time *The Sunday Times Magazine* was the only medium in which creative people could publish super colour ads and be certain that their friends in other agencies would see them. Their voices were therefore loud and strong in its support. The annual party gently canvassed their continuing votes.

Happy to relate, even Lord Thomson's best laid plans occasionally go slightly a-gley. There was an occasion when Oliver Knox could not attend the birthday festivities as he was suffering with mastoids. Unwilling to see free champagne go begging, Martin McKeand took Oliver's invitation and came with me to The Carlton Tower. Few people in the agency could have been less desirable as gatecrashers than Martin. He was head of the agency's television department, responsible for making commercials, and thus by definition especially unlikely to direct any advertising towards *The Sunday Times*.

As we approached the entrance to the party Martin Mc-Keand's enthusiasm for the priceless champagne dwindled. Standing at the door was a massive red-coated Master of Ceremonies deafeningly announcing each new arrival's name. The other side of the MC was Lord Thomson, shaking his guests warmly by the hand and welcoming them to his party. Martin dared not give his name as Oliver Knox: there were dozens of people present who knew he wasn't, and it was anyway quite possible that Lord Thomson—who had indeed met Oliver Knox previously—might recognize him as an impostor. Martin tried to back away from the entrance but the pressure of the crowd surging into the party pushed him forward. I stood behind him as, nervously still searching about him for some way of escape, he whispered to the Master of Ceremonies, 'I've come in place of Mr. Knox, who's got mastoids.'

'MISTER KNOX-MASTOIDS,' barked the MC in his most stentorian tones and Martin was catapulted towards Lord Thomson.

The good lord grasped his hand firmly, peered at Martin through his thick lenses and, exuding all the grateful affection of the true salesman said, 'Good evening, Mr. Mastoids. I'm *so* glad to be able to meet you again this year. Thank you *so* much for coming.'

Media 'medium' myths are those which are based on unproven hypotheses about the particular nature of each individual medium. For example:

> Television pre-empts attention for intrinsically uninteresting products.
> You can only tell a complicated story in print.
> Posters are a 'reminder' medium.

The third category of media myths, media 'message' myths, owe their name to McLuhan and their existence to admen's preconceptions and prejudices:

Women are more receptive to fashion ads in women's magazines than in daily papers.

Women have a personal relationship with women's magazines which increases the effectiveness of the ads.

The Times has authority, which it imparts to the ads it carries.

The Financial Times has authority, which it imparts to the ads it carries.

The Daily Telegraph/Sunday Times/Observer/Economist, etc. has authority, which...

Television has authority, which...

Obviously most of these myths have a basis in commonsense. They are not necessarily silly; they are unproven. Moreover they frequently contradict each other, so that an agency media director with an agile mind can always powerfully defend almost any schedule he likes to propose—with apparently irrefutable logic.

The fundamental problem is that we do not know enough about how advertisements work; we now know that there are interactions between advertisements and the media in which they appear; we don't know whether they occur always or sometimes, or when they work or how.* Most of the time we treat media purely as a vehicle: we assume that an impact is an impact, a message is a message. We assume that the more messages we can deliver for any given sum of money, the more efficient our schedule will be. To help media men plan schedules on this assumption, we have effective research techniques which give us fairly accurate quantitative data. How many people read any particular publication, how many people watched any particular television programme and so on. It is when we consider the medium as a medium rather than simply as a vehicle, as itself an intrinsic part of the message, that the inadequacies of existing media thinking

---

* Alan Smith's pioneering research for IPC Magazines, reported in his paper 'The Presenter Effect. Or Does The Medium Affect The Message?' establishes beyond doubt that the interaction exists, defines clearly the limits of our present knowledge, and establishes the research techniques that can be used to solve the problems.

become painfully obvious. We all know that we react to the same stimuli differently on Saturday night and on Sunday morning. We are bound to be affected differently by commercials shown during a break in the Morecambe and Wise Show and during a documentary on Auschwitz. We think differently of ads scrawled illiterately on walls and of ads occupying whole pages in the *Daily Express*. The magic words 'As Advertised on TV' bear witness to the powerful influence of the medium, quite distinct from that of the message.

Ah, says the sagacious media man, but those are imponderables. We cannot measure them arithmetically. That is why we calculate mathematically what can be calculated and create myths to cope with the rest. But this need not be the situation. The questions could be answered if time and money were spent; and if dissatisfied media men started to ask the fundamental questions once again.

While simultaneously seducing those who create the ads, with champagne and flattery, Lord Thomson was also holding intimate private luncheons in Thomson House for agency top people. Starting, I imagine, with J. Walter Thompson and working downward, the board and senior media executives of each agency were invited to meet Lord Thomson, Mark Boxer, then editor of *The Sunday Times Magazine,* and other Thomson Newspaper dignitaries. Lord Thomson was fully briefed on all of his guests before they arrived, conversed knowledgeably about their clients and their advertising problems, and casually neglected to promote *The Sunday Times Magazine* at all.

That's the way to sell media to advertisers.

A hazard commonly encountered by media departments is the de-escalating budget. All clients indulge in de-escalating budgets when corporate financial needs so dictate. After the campaign has been finalized, even after it has started, the client calls a meeting and—as if the light of some new eternal truth has just been revealed to him—with counterfeit naïveté he asks: 'If we were going to achieve our target sales with a £1,000,000 (or £10,000) campaign, surely it won't ruin everything if we only spend £950,000 (£9,500)?'

There is no crushing riposte to this. Who knows whether 9.5 impacts will have 80 per cent or 99 per cent of the sales effectiveness of 10.0 impacts in any particular case? The danger is that once a company's financial director has successfully argued that £950,000 is all but the same as £1,000,000 he can easily argue that £900,000 is all but the same as £950,000. So what is the difference between £850,000 and £900,000? And so on. That is how budgets de-escalate. I know of only one good argument against de-escalating budgets, the aeroplane analogy. 'Yes,' replies the media man to the client, 'and it is certainly true that if one engine is switched off, a four-engined aeroplane will fly, even if less effectively, on its remaining three. But turn off yet another engine and the plane may fall out of the sky.'

In advertising we never know which will be the critical engine to switch off. Nor precisely how much money can be cut from a budget before the campaign will fall out of the sky.

When you start in advertising it is very difficult to get media budgets in their proper perspective. Working on major consumer-goods accounts you quickly find yourself spending thousands, tens of thousands and even hundreds of thousands of pounds. It is very difficult, but essential, to keep reminding yourself that it is real money. Personally, you have probably never had more than a few pounds in your current account; each time you write a cheque for more than fifty quid you suffer an increase in your adrenalin level and minor palpitations of the heart. Yet you find yourself in meetings nonchalantly discussing whether to spend a mere £100,000 or maybe £200,000 as if it were Monopoly money.

The art is to sail safely between the Scylla of being too terrified by the huge sums involved and the Charybdis of being too cavalier about spending them. Most admen and brand managers sail dangerously close to the whirlpool of perfunctory casualness. Because the money apparently belongs to 'nobody', it is dangerously easy to throw around.

After £300,000 had been spent on Admiral cigarettes and had disappeared without a trace, I remember wondering: who has suffered? The newspapers and television companies had received just over £250,000 which no doubt helped them pay a few salaries and make a little more profit; the agency had received just under £50,000 with which it had done likewise. The Imperial Tobacco Company had 'lost' £300,000—but that's a fleabite off its profits, and its dividend to shareholders was not affected. A little less money went into ITCo's reserves, a little more money went into other people's. Who had suffered?

Of course, the answer is that time and effort had been wasted, human resources had been destroyed. It is difficult to appreciate that, when you are a small cog in a massive machine, spending other people's money without even seeing a cheque—let alone real cash—change hands.

That is why it is extremely salutary for admen to work from time to time with entrepreneurs who own their companies and who are spending their very own loot.

Christopher Collins, at Goya, is an enthusiast for high-frequency small-space campaigns. He may spend as much as £100,000 in a year on 6-inch single-column ads. When I first handled his account he 'phoned me to point out that the block in a particular 6-inch ad was only 5½ inches deep. 'That,' he reminded me, 'is over 8 per cent of the cost of the ad. £8,000 in a year could be wasted that way.'

There is one area of advertising where media schedules can be, and are, constantly and carefully scrutinized and assessed: direct-response advertising, advertising using coded coupons, the results of which can be accurately measured. At least £15 million is spent each year on direct-response advertising, almost 7 per cent of all display advertising in the Press. But for some reason direct-response advertising is the ugly sister of glamorous, immeasurable, branded consumer-product advertising. In Simon Broadbent's *Spending Advertising Money*, direct-response advertising merits half a page out of 258; in John Hobson's classic *The Selection of Ad-*

vertising Media, it doesn't even get an index mention, nor in David Ogilvy's nor Rosser Reeves's famous works. And E. J. Ornstien's excellent book *Mail Order Marketing* passed almost unnoticed in the Trade Press.

The curious thing is that many of the proven rules of mail order advertising are in total opposition to our established unproven beliefs about brand advertising. Here are a few examples:

(i) Small spaces are almost always more economical than large ones (reading and noting figures say the same of course), yet most media charge more per single column inch for large spaces than for small, and still manage to sell more than enough large space.

(ii) Response falls in direct ratio to frequency of insertion; yet every agency media department has its own myths about the 'minimum frequency necessary to achieve any impact'—and on television this is usually claimed to be at least two or three impressions a week.

(iii) Colour is almost never as economical as black and white; why then the mushrooming growth of expensive colour advertising and colour media?

(iv) Copy gets tired quickly and needs to be changed frequently (though there are some very rare examples of ads which apparently go on pulling, at a low frequency of insertion, for ever); what then, one wonders, was the basis for Rosser Reeves's famous dictum* that the client and the agency always get tired of a campaign long before the public do?

There is no reason to believe that all advertising works in the same way. Brand advertising is not intended to achieve quite the same results as direct-response advertising. Nevertheless all forms of advertising exist to sell; and it seems odd that we tend so much to ignore the one area where hard facts on how advertising works are available. It almost seems as if advertising people prefer to keep themselves to areas where nothing definite can be known; as if, having with difficulty acclimatized themselves to dealing with the un-

---

* In *Reality in Advertising*, Alfred A. Knopf, 1961.

certainties and vagaries of most advertising, they then wish to avoid the discipline that accurate measurement of the effectiveness of their work involves.

John Hughes of Hobson, Bates and Partners in a witty, scathing speech to the Market Research Society listed some of the inadequacies in current media research. First, Press readership information—which comes from the media man's bible, the massive and continuous National Readership Survey—is always an average of eleven months out of date. The demographic definitions in the NRS are hopelessly antiquated. Certain of the readership figures, particularly those for monthly magazines, are a total nonsense because of an unsolved technical problem called replication. Neither the techniques nor the size of the sample used by the NRS cope half-adequately with the readerships of small circulation up-the-market papers such as *The Times*. In the area of television viewership, there is almost no data on how and what people view in 'overlap' areas (areas of the country where viewers can receive and therefore choose between two different ITV programmes). The last effective research on the *attention* people pay to commercials was carried out over ten years ago. And no work has been done on the effect on commercials of the programmes in which they appear. As for posters—the paucity of the information available leaves us all happily in a state of total, blissful, uncomplicated ignorance.

As media men have become aware of the deficiencies in media research and media planning theory over the last few years, there has been a shift in emphasis in agency media departments. The trend has moved away from elaborate computer analyses and towards tougher buying and bargaining. You may not be absolutely certain that you're buying the right thing, runs the argument, but buy it as cheaply as possible.

The media, or at least the weaker, hungrier Press media, have responded by cutting their rates, giving free insertions, offering special positions at standard prices, allowing extra discounts, supplying free merchandising materials and other give-away goodies. Which in turn have made the computer analyses more meaningless still, based as they must be on published card rates (which are rarely adhered to).

Most advertising is being carefully and intelligently placed, many successful campaigns are being run. Nevertheless, as every media director since advertising agencies were invented has repeated: if media buying could be made just 10 per cent more cost-efficient, clients would save a great deal of money.

7 Client Hunting

Prospective clients are like prospective girl-friends. Until you know a girl quite well it is self-defeating to try too hard. As it is with new business. Nobody likes being chased too much. Most businessmen do not like being taken out to lunch or dinner too often by agency men who simulate undying friendship while metaphorically touching their knee under the table. Once the advertising trade Press has announced that an account is loose, unless you happen personally to know someone working in the client company there is no point in chasing it. Half the agencies in town will be doing likewise, and the likelihood is that you will end up wasting a lot of money, effort and precious time presenting to clients whom the odds are 100 to 1 against winning; money, effort and time that could be better spent improving the agency's service to its existing clients.

Ninety-nine per cent (or more) of the innumerable self-extolling mailing shots that agencies send to other agencies' clients are counter-productive. An agency which shall be nameless once mailed a promotional brochure to the late Douglas Collins when he was at Goya. Unlike many, Douglas did not throw mailing shots into the waste-paper basket unread. He appraised the brochure carefully and replied to the agency in roughly this vein:

Dear ——
As a client I have always been well aware that it is the unimaginative, dead hand of clients which kills so much of the brilliant and original creative work advertising agencies produce. It is therefore with particular interest that I study the literature that agencies themselves send me. Here, after all, they are their own clients. No out-

sider interferes with the copy and layout, no small-minded worries water down the original bold conception. From the outside front cover of your most interesting brochure I see that you have a front door. This certainly reassures me. I have never dealt with an advertising agency without a front door. I imagine it could be most inconvenient. Turning to the inside pages, I see that you have a Board of Directors and an organization. Good. Thoroughly commendable. I cannot say that the Directors' faces, which you reproduce on page 3 move me one way or the other. They are certainly not nasty faces, of the kind that one would feel unhappy at meeting late at night in a dark alley.

On pages 4 and 5 I see from the photographs that you employ secretaries. Sound thinking...

And so on. In a few paragraphs Douglas happily pinpointed what is wrong with almost every agency mailing shot. What is there new to say about an agency that hasn't already been said by every agency in history? The directors are wise and witty and widely experienced. The creative department are long-haired and wonderfully original but they really do care about sales. The partners take a personal interest in all of their clients, the media department buys television time more cheaply than any in London, the agency is international and has innumerable subsidiaries or doesn't believe in having any subsidiaries at all. Here is a list of our clients, here are our ads. We are truly lovely people.

Produced straightforwardly and tastefully—which they surprisingly rarely are—agency promotional brochures do little harm. They may occasionally do a little good. Clients, even advertising managers whose job it is to keep abreast of the current agency scene, are mostly unfamiliar with the great majority of agencies. After all, there are about four hundred to keep track of. Some clients therefore diligently keep a file of advertising agency brochures. That is the limit of their usefulness.

As well as producing expensive brochures, many large agencies employ expensive new-business-getters. At first sight this seems like a realistic, indeed necessary, job function—management consultants invariably recommend that every agency should have one. Unfortunately it is a ghastly, enervating job, requiring colossal physical, mental and emotional stamina. Physical energy is burnt up in the endless entertainment of prospective clients; mental energy is burnt up in the continuous effort to digest, understand and master new and complex marketing problems; emotional energy is burnt up both by the ever-smiling personal salesmanship, and by the repeated failures, since most accounts fought for are—in the nature of things—not won.

In the unhappy but fortunately unlikely event of the job being inflicted upon you, the only possible way to survive is to treat it cavalierly. Recently down from Oxford, Tim Miller was appointed new business executive at Sharps. Mark Ramage gave him a long and thorough briefing, detailing exactly what the job entailed.

'Aren't you taking notes?' Ramage asked towards the end of briefing.

'That hardly seems necessary. You are.'

Tim is now creative director of Mitford Advertising.

For a new agency, there is a danger in getting known too quickly. Particularly if you start pitching to a large number of clients as soon as you open the doors for business. If you pitch to clients when they are not looking for a change of agency you force them to say 'No'. Just as you do if you pitch to a girl who is happily enamoured of someone else. Once people have firmly said 'No', they rarely change their minds. When the time does come for that client to look for a new agency, he is more likely to move on and look at others, rather than to come back to one he has half-considered and rejected.

This has tripped up many new agencies in the last few years. They get off to a flying start with a few accounts. Feeling that they must strike while the iron is hot and that there is a tide in the affairs of men, they rush out mailing shots, hold lunches and dinners and parties, go for every bit of publicity they can get. Within three or four years almost every major client has been forced to consider them, and decided. Against.

It is very tempting to spend a lot of time pursuing new business. No moment in agency life is as exhilarating as the moment when you learn you have won a major new account. Conversely, no moment is as depressing as when you learn that you have lost one. A succession of new client presentations keeps staff morale high, makes everyone in the agency feel wanted. It combines the thrill of the chase with the chance to grow rich quick. But it can easily degenerate into a waste of energy and time.

A perfect example of how to grow steadily and successfully is Collett, Dickenson, Pearce. For many years they eschewed publicity. They turned down more business than they accepted. They went for clients for whom they could produce outstanding advertising. They let it be known that they would only accept new clients at a rate at which they could properly accommodate them, about two a year. It's an old trick in the agency game, but it always works.

Building an advertising agency is much more like building a solicitor's practice than like building a branded product. A few people choose a solicitor because they have read of him or heard of him. Most choose someone they know, or someone to whom they have been personally recommended. Word-of-mouth publicity is the most powerful of all agency-building techniques. That is why it is so much more important to give your existing clients better advertising than they could get anywhere else than to waste time chasing every rumour of a loose account that flies round the Coach and Horses.

While it is a mistake to chase uninterested clients too dedicatedly, once a prospective client has shown some interest and has intrepidly crossed your agency's threshold, it is impossible to try hard enough. Once a client has openly asked you to pitch for his business he is looking for and expects eagerness, dash and hard work. If there is a single word which summarizes all that most clients want from a new agency it is *enthusiasm*. That is almost invariably what has been missing at the old agency. Familiarity may have bred contempt; or a series of battles over the agency's creative work may have rotted the relationship; or constant agency reorganizations may have implied that nobody gave a damn about the client's business. Whatever the ostensible symptoms of trouble, the underlying malady can almost always be diagnosed as a lack of agency enthusiasm.

The best way to show enthusiasm is by showering the client with outlandish but just feasible ideas which might increase the sales of his product. The KMPH Partnership are masters of this technique. They gained Regent Petrol, one of their first really big accounts, by dressing all their secretaries in Regent symbol T-shirts (their own design) at the initial presentation and by having their receptionist greet the visiting Regent princes, standing with her foot on a tiger's head. (There were tigers in every Esso tank at the time.)

Ever since then KMPH have looked for some similar gimmick to catch each prospective client's imagination. When they were after a beer account they ingeniously arranged for a poster showing the agency's proposed campaign to be posted on a site outside the brewery, while the presentation of the same campaign was taking place at the agency's offices in Thorn House. The brewers, on returning from the presentation would see the campaign *in situ*. What could be more enthusiastic than that?

At Thorn House, KMPH waited for the client to arrive. Nobody came. Eventually an irate brewer telephoned to say that a poster he had never seen before, that he had not approved, and that he particularly disliked had been posted uninvited outside his offices, that he had traced the source of the unwanted advertisement to KMPH and would they please remove it immediately. The best laid plans ...

One of the very largest London agencies budgeted £45,000 to invest in the winning of a major international airline account. A perfectly reasonable sum for an account billing £3,000,000 around the world. At 1½ per cent, considerably less in percentage terms than many agencies spend on new business presentations. Rather less than is frequently spent in other industries in securing contracts of a similar size. But a large sum of money all the same.

Two days before the presentation someone in the agency realized that they had only spent £43,000 on the project. 'If,' he said, 'we don't get the account, we'll be blamed by the boss for not having spent up to budget. It will look as if we didn't try hard enough.' So they went out and bought the agency £2,000 of photographic equipment. It didn't win them the account.

There is a good deal of hogwash talked and written about speculative creative presentations for new clients. As three generalizations: advertising agencies are against creative presentations; the bigger the agency the more hostile it is likely to be; many clients are against them in theory but ask for them when the time comes.

The only good argument against speculative creative presentations is that they stop the agency's best people from working on existing clients' campaigns. This is argued to be foolish at best, immoral at worst. All of which is nonsense. Any agency which cannot cope with the strains and stresses of a peak workload at short notice ought not to be in business. There are no senior creative men in London who work only on one account. They all work on seven or eight or many more. If six of their clients all need a new campaign at once they have to work bloody hard. If a new client comes in the same day they have to work still harder. They may then pass a fortnight in comparative idleness and long lunch hours. Violent oscillations of pace and effort are the nature of the agency business. Tidy-minded people who prefer their life to be of an even tenor should work in a bank.

The honest reason why agencies are against producing speculative creative work is that it costs money. Sometimes very large sums of money. Although some clients offer to reimburse agencies for any speculative work they do, this rarely comes near to covering the real cost. That is why bigger agencies are more hostile to speculative creative presentations than smaller agencies. Bigger agencies, competing against each other for bigger accounts, are forced to spend bigger sums of money. Ogilvy, Benson and Mather executives keep making speeches calling for a moratorium on speculative creative work, with all agencies agreeing not to produce any. Fortunately, in our fiercely competitive world it will never happen. If it did it would be an illegal agreement in restraint of trade. Nobody likes spending money on presenting for new business. It is much nicer if an account comes in without the agency spending a dime. But if I were a client I might well ask for speculative creative presentations, to help me make a very difficult decision: which agency would be best for my business?

At Sharps we aimed to show enthusiasm by carrying out a detailed market research survey of the prospective client's products and presenting him with the results when he visited the agency. This formula was partly based on the proposition that Sharps was one of the few smallish agencies which owned a really first-class market-research subsidiary, and this gave us a competitive advantage; and partly based on the fact that Mark Ramage happens to like carrying out market research, rather preferring it to producing advertisements, since the results give him new knowledge and stimulate his insatiable curiosity about products and markets.

I was against the formula on the twin grounds that our research—of necessity carried out quickly and cheaply—could never be as thorough as the client's own, so that we ran the risk of producing demonstrable inaccuracies; and that in any event we were trying to sell ourselves as an advertising agency and not as a market-research company.

On several occasions we did indeed get into arguments over our market-research results. If we showed the prospective client as having a smaller market share than he believed he had, the presentation was likely to take a sharp turn for the worse. Our most catastrophic presentation was to a well-known self-made tycoon who was then spending about £250,000 a year on advertising.

The tycoon had more faith in flair—of which he had a good deal—than in figures. Like most other tycoons he named his products after himself. Our research had shown that anyone who had owned a Tycoon product, or even knew anyone who had owned a Tycoon product, was likely to have a pretty poor opinion of it. The 7-point rating scales veered strongly towards 'Not Good Quality'. Fortunately all was not lost, however. The research showed that at that time the majority of the populace had still not heard of Tycoon, and therefore had neither favourable nor unfavourable opinions of either himself or of his products. Tycoon was no doubt well aware that the quality of his products was not perfect. Tycoon's products were very cheap; and you got what you paid for. He was therefore about to launch a rather better product at a slightly higher price.

In the light of the research our argument to him was to be a simple one: fortunately for you, most people still have not heard of you or of your products; you are now bringing out a better product; if the advertising majors on this it will help change the unfortunate image of Tycoon products held by that proportion of the population that does, in fact, know something about them.

The presentation began with Mark Ramage showing the first large chart:

> We asked a thousand housewives: Which makes of this
> kind of product have you heard of?
> President   88%
> King   51%
> Emperor   42%
> Pharaoh   33%
> TYCOON   26%

From behind his desk the tycoon exploded. 'Lies. All lies. Are you telling me that only twenty-six per cent of the people in the country have heard of my product? It's lies.'

'That...' Mark faltered; 'that's what the research shows, Mr. Tycoon.'

'Rubbish.' He pressed his intercom buzzer and called for his sales director.

'Who's the most famous manufacturer of our kind of product in this country?'

'Tycoon, Mr. Tycoon,' his sales director answered dutifully. (I swear that's what he said.)

'What percentage of the population know about our products?'

'Just about everyone, *I'd* say, Mr. Tycoon.'

'Exactly. Exactly. These advertising people have come round here with a bundle of lies trying to prove that only 26 per cent have heard of us. Take this morning. The taxi-driver recognized me. "Good morning, Mr. Tycoon," he said. There you are. What more proof do you want? I don't want to hear any more of your lies, Mr. Ramage. Please go. Get out. Now. NOW!'

There ended the presentation.

I always said that presenting market-research results was a risky business.

One good reason for not making too many new business presentations too quickly, is that this inevitably means stereotyping the agency pitch. Everyone knows that ideally every presentation should be individually hand-tailored for the particular prospective client involved. As advertising movies have frequently shown, the agency should try to discover *everything* about the prospect: his product, his markets, his politics, his religion, his taste in wines, girls, cigars, underwear and lavatory paper.

When at MCR we were pitching for Kimberley-Clark business, an account we won, I remembered five minutes before the presentation was due to start that we did not have KC tissue in the loo. I dashed to the nearest chemist, unwilling to entrust my secretary with so urgent and crucial a task. By a stroke of good fortune the chemist stocked Kleenex rolls.

If you are pitching several times a week—and simultaneously trying to produce good advertising for your existing clients—there is not time for such close attention to important detail. As a result, instead of learning about the client and his problems the agency is forced to talk about itself and its philosophy. Several agencies in town—KMPH, The Kirkwood Company, Saatchi and Saatchi, Lippa, Newton —which purport to have special, new, exciting agency philosophies tend to do this. There are some clients who are fascinated by advertising-agency philosophies. They listen entranced when a new agency explains that it and it alone has no account executive, or no media department, or no teaboy or no ballpens. Such clients find agency organization charts things of beauty and joys forever. But they are a minority. Most clients don't really give a damn how their agency is organized, any more than they care very much about how their printers or their solicitors are organized. They care about the end product, their advertising. It is the agency's job to ensure that it is outstanding. How the agency does it is its own business.

Immediately an important new business presentation ends and the client has left, everyone from the agency breaks into nervous chatter, squawking like parrots.

'How do you think it went? How do you think it went? How do you think it went?'

'Did you notice that bloody product manager yawning?'

'I think the marketing director was for us. They certainly liked the ads. Do you think they liked the ads? I think they liked the ads. What do you think?'

'That guy with the moustache hated us. I know he did. I could see it. He's got a friend at Benton and Bowles.'

'Do you think we've got it or not? Do you? Do you?'

Mark Ramage and I presented for a small food account. It was unlikely to be profitable but we wanted a food account badly. As soon as they had left the usual self-interrogation began.

'How do you think it went?' I asked Mark.

'Not bad. Not bad at all.'

'I think it went pretty well.'

'I should say that we were in with a chance.'

'Mind you, they were a stupid pair,' I said. 'God knows how we're going to deal with them. Bags I not be account director. I just can't cope with clients as stupid as that.'

'Do you think,' asked a voice from the door quietly, 'that I might have my raincoat? I left it behind. Sorry to have interrupted you.'

That is the only inviolable rule of new business presentations. When the presentation is over and you think the client has gone, shut up.

8 *On the Doorstep*

Whether or not there is more promiscuous sex in advertising agencies than elsewhere I am not qualified to say. I doubt it. At Selfridges, where I worked on and off for fifteen months, everyone was a great deal more preoccupied—and occupied—with sex than at any of the three agencies in which I have worked. I know of at least as many unfaithful clients as unfaithful agency men. As many faithful ones too.

Agencies have their share of unfaithful lunchtime lovers, stationery cupboard copulators, secretary seducers and leaving party libertines. Their share, but no more. The exiguous hideaways in office blocks and factories where couples find the time and space to couple are unsung triumphs of basic human ingenuity. Agency art directors have more opportunities than most, because of the procession of models desirous of employment who pass through their offices and lives. But no more opportunity than Henry Miller would have us believe the average personnel manager enjoys.

I myself have never believed in the necessity to avoid dirtying one's own doorstep, as the nasty cliché has it. I have never believed in it, but I have always been scared it might be true. All of my office romances have therefore been cloaked in absurd secrecy. The most secret and most absurd of all being the four years pre-marital romance with my wife. We worked at Sharps together. Our relationship was one long subterfuge. No doubt this added to the excitement. We would get on and off buses at different stops. We would arrive at the cinema separated by a ten-minute interval and meet at the popcorn kiosk. I would linger for a quarter of an hour to avoid leaving the office with her. She would walk to Piccadilly Circus Station while I went to nearby Green Park, so that we would be seen separating on the corner of Albemarle Street and Piccadilly.

One evening Paddy Ross, an account executive at Sharps, returned to the offices late at night when she and I were still there together, behaving quite innocently. She was working late and I was hanging about waiting. Unable to think of an excuse for being in the building at that time of night—everybody knew I had lately been rather slack—I hid in a cupboard on the stairs. Paddy heard the noise and asked Jean if there was anyone else in the building. She said she thought not. Paddy came out on to the staircase and lunged bravely at the cupboard door, throwing it open, expecting no doubt to discover Jack the Ripper. I fell out of the cupboard, feigning drunkenness. 'Hull, Padgy. I'm playing a liddle game. Gonna frighten Jean. D'you wanna play with me?' Acting has never been my strong point, but he was sufficiently convinced and he guided me gently out of the building into a taxi and home. Where I waited for Jean.

It was all dotty. Doubly dotty because half the agency knew about us but generously feigned ignorance so that we could continue to play our charade. Unfortunately this meant that we were never quite certain who knew and who did not.

Norman Griffiths took Jean to dinner one evening and made a friendly unpersistent pass at her. Having had a certain amount to drink at dinner, she thought it would be amusing to fob him off with a tale of desperate unrequited love. 'I cannot respond to your affections,' she said (or at least she says she said), 'because I am deeply in love with Winston and he will not even deign to look at me. Woe is me, woe is me, my heart is breaking, what am I to do?' She had been going around with me for over six months at the time.

A week later, Norman tackled me on a train coming back from a Player's meeting in Nottingham. 'You are a bastard', he said suddenly and out of the blue.

'Why, what do you mean?' I was his assistant, and one does not like to be called a bastard by one's boss. It is unlikely to be a signal for promotion or be good for one's career.

'You know that girl is pining for you.'

'Which girl?' I was beginning to cotton on.

'You know perfectly well. Jean Brownston. You're behaving like a shit to her.'

I defended myself in the only way I could think of. 'What are you talking about? When did she tell you all this?' A question he was unlikely to want to answer.

'Never mind. I just think you ought to stop behaving like a bastard.'

For some weeks I lived in slight fear that he would uncover Jean's jolly jape, and not be amused. Fortunately he didn't.

Despite my own ineptness in the matter, it is perfectly possible to keep an affair successfully clandestine in even the smallest and most gossip-ridden agency—so long as both parties are sufficiently discreet by nature. Time and again I have learned of liaisons months after they were over, neither I nor anyone else in the agency having known of them while they were in progress.

There was a girl I knew very well at Sharps, a respectable, rather prissy middle-class twenty-five-year-old secretary. She and I had lunch together at least once a week and often had a drink together after work, gossiping about the agency and the romances therein. It was not until some months after she left that I learnt she had all along been having an affair with one of my closest friends in the agency. Neither of them was married, so I am not certain to this day why they kept it all so dark; any more than I fully understand why I tried to keep my own entanglements well hidden. Perhaps nobody wishes to be the object of everyone else's gossip. Whatever the reason, in any agency you can be reasonably certain that several of such harmless furtive relationships will be going on at any one time.

About one clandestine romance per thirty staff is par for the course.

There are certain females that a young man seeking advancement in an advertising agency is well advised to cultivate. One is his boss's secretary. This need not involve a passionate love affair. A few beers in the pub at lunchtime once a week and a cuddly shuffle at the Christmas party will probably suffice. Another good prospect is any senior lady in the creative department. (There are rarely senior ladies in other departments.) Undeniably my own *affaire de cœur* with the art director helped my career greatly, though in all honesty I did not plan it that way. Whenever I had a rush job, or whenever I had made a howler (*vide* Player's Navy Cut Tobacco and the *Reader's Digest* ad), I could rely on Jean saving my bacon. Even when the going was smooth and efficient, I could rely on my work—that is, my client's work—being done quickly and well. So my clients thought I was a splendid fellow. And said so.

Although they loom large in business fiction and in television plays, I have never thought the boss's wife a good catch. Firstly, of course, developing such a liaison must be extraordinarily dangerous. Secondly, and more relevantly from an ambitious young man's point of view, businessmen rarely talk to their wives about business—rightly assuming that their wives find the subject ineffably boring. Thirdly, the odds are at least two to one that anything a wife says her husband will disagree with, and that any young man she riskily praises her husband will promptly decide is a nincompoop.

All the same rules apply, in equal but opposite directions, to ambitious young ladies.

It is fascinating to speculate why the prejudice against dirtying one's own doorstep is so widely held in business, while marrying the girl next door occupies such an esteemed position in novelette mythology. David Ogilvy states emphatically that immediately two of his staff get married one of them has to leave. Preferably the wife, he says rather coyly, to breed. Obviously love affairs can complicate business life. Both while they last and, more specifically, when they stop. While the relationship exists, each partner will be unreliable *vis-à-vis* the other: there will be favouritism, and it could be difficult to fire either one of them should this be necessary. Confidential information will be shared.

But think of all the advantages, from the company's point of view. The couple are certain to spend much of their time discussing work. S. J. Perelman relates how in the 1930's Hollywood Moguls preferred to employ husband-and-wife writer teams because they could rely on the couple continuing to work together on their scripts late into the night when otherwise they might have been otherwise engaged. Thus the Mogul would get double value for the mean salaries he paid. A couple working together are likely to be doubly loyal; and one of them is unlikely to leave for fear of damaging the other's position. The obverse of favouritism is that their joint work is likely to be quickly and efficiently done. And if and when the wife finally does heed David Ogilvy's advice and leaves to breed, she will continue to understand and be interested in her husband's work. It's the great advantage of marrying your secretary. But then I am obviously biased.

Like nepotism, it all depends on how it is handled. For many years I was strongly antagonistic to nepotic appointments in business. I expressed my views to Joe Hyman, one-time king of Viyella International—then our client at Sharps—and a self-made millionaire several times over, who had recently appointed one of his close relatives to be managing director of a Viyella subsidiary.

'It's all good sentimental stuff,' I said, 'jobs for the boys. Charity begins at home. Keeps the Jewish family together and all that. But I can't help believing that somewhere among the fifty million or so inhabitants of Great Britain there is someone better qualified to do that job than your relative. And it would be in the interests of your shareholders for you to employ that somebody.'

'My dear boy,' Joe replied unmoved, 'you don't seem to understand how business works. It isn't because they're so fond of their families that Jewish businessmen employ their nearest and dearest. Why do you think Sir Jack Cohen has his family in Tesco? Why are there so many Marks and Sieffs in Marks and Spencer? Why is Lyons full of Salmons? I could point to dozens of successful family firms, Jewish and non-Jewish. Until a few years ago there was never a non-

Rothschild on the Rothschild board. You'll never be a director of C & A if you're not a Brenninkmeyer.'

'Just because a few companies practise nepotism successfully does not prove it's the best way to run a business.'

'It's how it's done that matters. Not *whether* it's done. Look,
supposing I hadn't given that managing directorship to my
relative. I needed someone to fill the job. I would have gone
to a management selection company. At the end of two
months they would have given me a short list of three. I'd
have interviewed each candidate for maybe an hour, if I
could spare the time. Then I would have chosen the one I
liked best. Almost a pig in a poke. Then I spend a year getting to know his strengths and weaknesses, treating him
gently, learning where I can rely on him, where I can't, and
at the end of twelve months I discover he's no good or I
can't work with him so I fire him and start again. Instead
of all that palaver I employ a close relative. Just because a
chap is on the doorstep doesn't prove he's no good. I know
my relative's abilities. I know when to look over his shoulder.
I know he's a born optimist so I cut all his estimates by
20 per cent. And you know you can be a lot nastier and
tougher to relatives than to strangers. You can tell a relative
exactly what you think of him much more easily than you
can tell someone you've just employed. Nepotism can be a
very effective form of management. If you handle it right.'

Nepotism is like sex in ads and agency love affairs. It's not
what you do, it's the way that you do it that counts.

Whether or not there is more sex in advertising agencies
than in other industries, there is definitely less sex in advertisements than in our permissive society generally. Nobody outside of advertising believes this; but a few unbiased
evenings spent watching television commercials or reading
women's magazines will confirm it. Advertisements are far
more conservative about sex than are the mass media in
which they appear. Advertisements are mostly as sexless and
impotent as eunuchs. A few, a very few advertisements show
nudes, nearly always modestly nippleless. A few promise

sexual success, of a painstakingly vague and unspecific kind. Occasionally an advertisement gets to press portraying something sexy; invariably it is quickly withdrawn.

Freud or one of his disciples claimed that the phallic stance of church steeples was evidence of the underlying sexuality of religion. The theory is reminiscent of the old joke about the patient who accuses his analyst of having a mind like a sewer: 'You see a dirty meaning in everything I say.'

So it is with advertising. A few years ago I attended a meeting of a left-wing Study Group on Advertising. I had seen the meeting advertised on the back page of the *New Statesman*. It was held in a room above a pub in the West End. I went along, not knowing what to expect, honestly hopeful that my inside knowledge might be helpful to the group's studies. The meeting was a predictable caricature of a left-wing Study Group on Advertising. There were about a dozen people present, all workers with ballpen and brain; all with their own personal, pernickety, paranoiac phobias of particular aspects of advertising. One rather kindly elderly man in a woolly check shirt and tweed tie was obsessed with the immorality of army recruitment ads. A rotund lady in a flowered cotton dress, who I guessed to be a school teacher, was preoccupied with violence in commercials and the effects on children. A chap in a lounge suit with a stiff collar and old-school tie delivered a brief but violent masterpiece of rhetorical invective against booze advertising. I would not have guessed him to be capable of such passion. I wondered if he had closed his eyes and thought of England on his journey through the pub downstairs en route to the meeting.

There appeared to be no chairman, and each of the participants mounted his own private hobby-horse in turn, ignoring what had been said before. Eventually, however, they seemed to find a common cause: sex in advertising, the huge volume and deplorable nature thereof. Suddenly, to demonstrate the insidious way that sex creeps into advertising everywhere, a man pulled an ad out of his pocket and read the copy, in tones tremulous with anger and excitement. 'To make Navy Cut Tobaccos we lay a group of tobacco leaves lengthwise together and . . .' (here I feared for the strain he was putting on his vocal chords as he screamed) *'we bind them with a rope until they go hard.'*

I almost fell from my rickety, folding chair. I had written those words myself at a meeting with a client a few months before. They were the end result of hours of literary struggle, during which we had endeavoured to describe as clearly and concisely as possible the very traditional manufacturing process that is still used to make Navy Cut Tobaccos. Sex, I swear, had never entered our heads. The damn sentence was difficult enough to write, without trying to build into it titillating and extraordinarily perverse ambiguities.

Until that moment I had stayed silent throughout the confused proceedings. Then I exploded. I attempted in five incoherent minutes to meet and refute all the more non-sensical arguments that had been raised in the previous two hours. Nobody, I insisted, and least of all I, wishes to wash advertising whiter than white. Advertising is in many ways an inefficient, occasionally wasteful and very occasionally immoral activity. But if improvements are to be made, in-formed logic and intelligence must prevail; neurotic fears of sex rearing its head from every billboard and matchbox cover are irrelevant and unhelpful. It was to no avail of course. If you want to believe that church steeples have a dirty meaning, nothing will ever convince you otherwise.

There are many reasons why ads are rarely sexy. The rules controlling the content of advertisements are far stricter than those the media apply to themselves. Advertisers, wishing to sell their products as widely as possible, try to avoid offend-ing any of the people any of the time. Though we use lots of products to enhance our sex appeal, we use very few for sex for itself—so that sex *per se* is irrelevant in most advertise-ments. Moreover on those rare occasions when it appears, it is so much more interesting than the product itself that con-sumers are most likely to end up remembering the sex but forgetting the product. If advertisements exert any influence at all on sexual morals, which is doubtful, their influence is Victorian, prudish and chaste.

None of which will go very far to placate determined

supporters of Women's Lib. Almost all Women's Liberation-
ists are hostile to advertising. They raise two main areas of
complaint. Firstly that women are treated in advertisements
as sexual objects to be lusted after, portrayed without in-
dividuality or humanity, using the most aphrodisiac bras or
lipsticks. Alternatively, that women are treated in advertisements as doormats, suburban nonentities who exist only to
stuff their husbands' and children's faces full of frozen foods,
to scrub the floors, do the washing and keep the lavatory
clean.

To answer Women's Lib complaints, it is first essential to
differentiate between those ads which in themselves could
be insulting to women, and those which accurately portray
the way things now happen to be. Commercials which show
housewives chatting about detergents and admiring the white-
ness of a wash obviously imply that washing is women's work.
But then in our society it is. To show men discussing the
washing—what would Gay Lib say about that?—would be
ludicrous.

When I handled the Sun Valley Handrolling Tobacco
account, we received a letter every year from an enthusiastic
lady Sun Valley user, complaining that we never showed
women rolling their own. She claimed to know many lady
handrollers, and she offered to model. Each year we regret-
fully rejected her generous offer. Not because, as I am sure
she came to believe, we were anti-feminist but because women
—except for a tiny minority—don't handroll. And men—
except for a tiny minority—don't do the washing.

Women's Lib supporters may argue that in accurately re-
flecting women's present role in society, advertisements help
to buttress the status quo. Some advertisements may do;
others—encouraging women (as well as men) to read more
newspapers is a simple example—certainly do not. In any
event the ways in which influences of this kind work are
extremely complex and nobody knows enough to start throwing around generalizations. We know little enough about the
ways in which advertisements influence people's attitudes to
the actual products being advertised.

If a product is manufactured with the sole object of making

females more sexually attractive, it is difficult to see how or why its advertising should avoid saying so. Maybe while burning their bras, some Women's Lib protagonists also want to melt down their lipsticks, ladder their stockings, shave their heads and drink their scents for the alcohol. If you happen to find cosmetic products objectionable you don't have to use them; the ads merely portray, as attractively as possible, what the products do. As ads, they can do little else.

Moving from the bedroom to the washing machine, it seems true and fair that a few—though only a very few—ads disparage women. There is a school of women-are-hopelessly-incompetent-but-we-love-'em-just-the-same ads. There is also the school of women-are-frightened-little-mice-without-a-big-strong-man-to-support-them ads. And thirdly there are the if-you-aren't-married-you-ought-to-be-ashamed-of-yourself-you failure ads (of which the classic example and prototype for innumerable unashamed plagiarisms, is Listerine's 'Why am I always the bridesmaid?'). You don't need to be an impassioned Women's Lib supporter to see that any educated, intelligent single woman might find these advertisements rude and insulting. The trouble is that such ads do strike a warm chord in the hearts of the majority. And ads are by their nature written and designed to speak to the majority. Mass-selling in mass-communications media is precisely what advertising is about.

Advertisements, speaking to millions of women at a time about products that millions use, must obviously 'stereotype' needs and emotions to a degree. Nor need there be anything wrong or unpleasant in that. Just because we all wear Marks and Spencer underwear does not make us dull and character-less.

Nevertheless, if advertising is to avoid a growing hostility from the ever-increasing number of independent, thinking women, many of whom are also active consumerists, we shall have to avoid producing ads of these kinds. While we're about it, we might try not to produce ads which offend men either. There are quite a few of those about, too.

9 Games Admen Play

There is a prevalent cliché that business is a game. This is twaddle. In the first place, games were invented to simulate life, rather than life invented to simulate games. In the second place, an activity which creates employment and unemployment, wealth and poverty, the corruptions of power and the distresses of nervous breakdown, bears little resemblance to Ludo. Which is not to say that businessmen do not play games. They play simple business games like Sandhurst toy-soldier wars, complex computerized business games like Pentagon atomic wars. They fight open battles in which all contestants are aware a tournament is taking place, and wage devious wars in which some of the combatants are unaware that hostilities have begun until they learn that they have lost.

Most admen describe their chosen business as a rat race —an odd neologism that: do rats really race?—and talk incessantly about unscrupulous bastards who get to the top by climbing on their weaker brethren's backs while trampling on their underlings' faces, who grind their competitors into the ground while delicately inserting scalpels into their spines and kneeing them in the groin. (Metaphors abound but often get a little mixed in the confusion of all those skirmishes.) Such admen see their careers as a continuous underground war, in which they fight for each promotion against back-stabbing enemies and untrustworthy friends. Viewing the world through blood-tinted spectacles they see a plethora of dog-fights and cock-fights and prize-fights, of bleeding noses and catch-as-catch-can with no holds barred, of guerilla warfare and blitzkreig and scorched earth. Every image of war is used; life is a battlefield.

Maybe I am naïve or blind, but I believe that the vast

majority of those at the top in advertising are rather nice, rather kind people, who have reached their lofty status because they are rather more able and rather more talented than their colleagues. I've met a few shits, but I can count them on the fingers of one hand. The successful people in ad agencies are certainly ambitious and extremely hard working; they think very quickly and, like politicians, foresee the inevitable consequences of their statements and actions, which often makes them seem cunning. But they are if anything too soft rather than ruthless, too kind rather than unscrupulous. Maybe I have been lucky, but I have seen extraordinary little cut-throat viciousness, little execrable behaviour. None of which is surprising in a business whose principal asset is clever people. The prime task of an agency manager is to get intelligent and often perverse people to work hard and enthusiastically for him. He is unlikely to be very good at this if he is a malevolent sod.

When agency men do try their hand at a bit of snaky scheming, their motives are usually so transparent and their manoeuvres so artless that even the most ingenuous client quickly sees through them.

At an early age I learned that give-the-client-a-good-lunch-before-you-show-him-the-ads is a very dangerous game and almost invariably rebounds in your face. Firstly, every client knows it. Secondly instead of becoming more well-disposed towards you after a few drinks, as the game presupposes, many people become more cantankerous. Thirdly, and most dangerous of all, is that in the unlikely event of a client approving, in a post-prandial spirit of bonhomie and goodwill, ads which he does not really like, he will hate them from the next morning onwards. Getting the artwork approved will be torture; every nit that can be found on the proofs will be picked; each time the ad appears in the Press or on the screen the client will suffer a short sharp twinge of hangover; eventually his account will go.

Oliver Knox developed, for a certain client, a more sophisticated version of this game which was intended to avoid its pitfalls. The particular client was extremely large, weighing over eighteen stone, and loved his food. Meetings were always fixed for noon so that he could see and approve (or disapprove) the agency's work in the hour before going off for his habitual massive midday feast.

Oliver Knox countered by packing the early part of every agenda with trivia, digressing lengthily on each of them, and using all of his considerable conversational wiles to ensure that any new ads which needed to be approved would not be shown before 1 p.m. By one o'clock the hungry client's mind would be on food glorious food. Anything that might delay the first morsels reaching his lips was to be avoided at all costs. Rejecting ads takes time and invariably involves long and tortuous arguments. If he wanted his grub quickly, the client had no alternative but to approve what was presented to him. Nor would he be likely to suffer future remorse on account of having approved the ads under the influence of alcohol.

For many months the game worked perfectly. Then the client twigged. We discovered this when the agency's production manager, enjoying a midday beer with a supplier, saw the client in the pub opposite our offices at ten minutes to twelve downing two pints of bitter and three rounds of beef prior to the meeting, prior to lunch. At one o'clock that day he took his time, and leisurely rejected all the ads.

Advertising is a fissiparous business. Agencies are forever splitting apart like amoeba on a slide. Every year at least a dozen hopeful new agencies spring up, each founded by two or three young men who believe that they have discovered the alchemists' magical formula for advertising success. All young admen worth their salt dream of one day opening their own shop. Endlessly they discuss the possibility in furtive whispers, over their beers in The Running Footman— where only about one third of the rest of the advertising world can hear them. Let's start an agency is a harmless game, which can pass many an idle hour happily.

The night that Eisenhower visited Macmillan, four of us sat in the boardroom watching the President and Prime Minister on television and imbibing the agency's whisky. Len

Deighton, then an art director at Robert Sharps, myself, Jean Brownston and Michael Kaye, another bright young graduate, now managing director of Sharps.

'Why,' someone brightly suggested, no doubt inspired to ambition by the sight of Our Two Great Leaders, 'don't we leave this crowd and set up on our own?'

'Do you think we could?' I had been in advertising about three months and had had two jobs already. Confident of my own talents though I was, it seemed a trifle premature to be starting an agency.

'All the talent in Sharps', Len said, 'is in this room. The only problem is what would we call ourselves?'

'Pass me the whisky.'

'You see it should be alphabetical—Brownston, Deighton, Fletcher and Kaye. But that would mean a girl first. Do you think that would matter? What about backwards alphabetical? Kaye, Fletcher, Deighton and Brownston. Don't like the rhythm. What do you think Michael?'

'I like Kaye being first, I think.'

'But it should have two syllables, the first word. It doesn't feel right, just one syllable. What about Fletcher, Deighton, Brownston and Kaye. That sounds good. Fletcher, Deighton, Brownston and Kaye. Very good that. Fletcher, Deighton, Brownston and Kaye. Let's have another drink....'

Norman Griffiths walked in at that moment. 'Listen Norman,' Len whispered confidentially, 'Jean and Michael and Winston and I are leaving Robert Sharps. Don't worry, we won't take any accounts. There's only one difficulty, what should our agency be called?'

'You won't take any accounts! How very generous of you. And which do you think you *could* take?' Norman inquired sarcastically.

But Len stuck doggedly to his point. 'It really *should* be alphabetical, but I think Deighton, Brownston, Kaye and Fletcher sounds better. Or do I mean Fletcher, Brownston, Deighton and Kaye or ... what did we agree just now, Winston? What was it? Deighton, Kaye ... what was it? Anyway what do you think, Norman? You're good at naming things....'

Let's Start An Agency is an addictive game, and the addiction is not cured by starting an agency. Shortly after starting an agency, withdrawal symptoms occur which can only be alleviated by playing the game in reverse. Thus while the young admen, in the pubs, are secretively plotting their breakaways, their elders, in their clubs, are simultaneously but even more secretively plotting mergers.

A good game for alleviating the tedium of long meetings is Drag the Word In. This is really a game for two but may be played by any number. When two play, each gives the other an unlikely word to bring naturally into conversation during the meeting. The first person to use his designated word is the winner. Words which seem promising often turn out not to be. Elephant, for example, is a simple word to drag by the scruff of its neck into any advertising discussion: 'This outstanding, creative, impactful campaign will be as powerful as an elephant charging through the jungle of competition.'

Or, less acceptably: 'Have you thought of an on-pack giveaway of a free plastic elephant?'

Asparagus is a good word, difficult to bring naturally into the average advertising discussion; so are blowpipe, briny, carboniferous, diathermal, raffia, turmeric and woollies. It's not difficult to think of thousands more. There are only two rules: every word chosen must be in the Shorter Oxford English Dictionary, and must be used relevantly, not shouted as a sudden expletive, e.g. 'Carboniferous, dammit!' or 'Woollies, I tell you, woollies!'

Applying this rule of course often calls for fine judgement, and the game can therefore only be played by Gentlemen of Honour, employing mutual trust and confidence.

Whether or not they can strictly be defined as games, Diplomatic Illnesses are endemic in the advertising business. They are usually the result of absent-minded double-booking: arranging meetings and/or lunches with two or more clients on the same day often at the same time, and sometimes even at the same place. Such arrangements inevitably produce moments of excitement and high drama—as when the temp telephonist tells your largest client that you are in your office having a cup of tea, while he believes you to be attending your maternal grandmother's funeral. Or when you are seen on television spectating at Wimbledon, having absented yourself from an important meeting with a smaller client, to play host to a larger one.

I frequently double-book myself, being mildly amnesiac. Keeping a diary is of some help but is not an infallible solution to the problem, since clients often insist on fixing meetings with my secretary in my absence. Theoretically, once such a dilemma has occurred it should be possible to explain the circumstances sensibly to one of the clients involved and move one of the meetings; and usually it is. But if each of the meetings involves, say, eight busy people who may be gathering together from all parts of the country to discuss a matter of urgent importance, eight people who may not all simultaneously be free and available again for several weeks, then it is extremely difficult to put either group off. Not that a diplomatic illness is a very satisfactory solution either. It's a Gordian knot I've never learned how to untangle.

A good game for art directors, models and photographers is Junctions. This is best played by a crowd of friendly people, together on location taking photographs or making a commercial, late at night.

The rules again are simple. The photographer always starts by naming the last person with whom he had an affair. Let's call that person Jemima Puddleduck. Then, by question and answer, each of the rest of the party tries to trace someone they themselves have had an affair with at some time in their lives, who in turn went with X, who in turn went with Y etc., until somebody builds a chain back to ... Jemima Puddleduck, thence to the photographer. The photographer and the member of the party linked with him—via Jemima

Puddleduck—both score a point. The individual, almost certainly not present, who joined both ends of the chain and is therefore responsible for the link is called a junction, but this is only of passing personal interest to the participants and is of no consequence whatsoever to the game itself.

Another member of the party then names his or her last paramour, and the tracing of the chain starts again. If no chain can be built no points are scored. After everyone present has named their last lover, the photographer starts again on his last but one, and so on. Among art directors, photographers and models the game can continue indefinitely. The winner is the person who scores most points.

I am not certain what prizes are normally awarded.

There are no rules which can guarantee success and victory in the computerized business games which are now so much in vogue. However there are certain principles to which it is wise to adhere. These are based on the oft-proven assumption that those who programme the computer games have read innumerable management textbooks but have minimal business experience. On this assumption, it is almost always advisable to adopt the following strategies when playing computer games:

To raise your prices sky-high.
To train and retain your sales reps whatever the cost.
To avoid running out of stock at all costs.
To spend heavily on all forms of marketing and promotion.
To borrow money at fixed interest whenever possible.

One of the most brilliantly successful companies I know is the Goya company run by Christopher Collins, whose policies are:
To keep prices at rock bottom.
To keep his sales reps on the road as much as possible.
To under-produce and run out of stock rather than over-produce and write off dead goods.

To spend the minimum on marketing promotion that will do the job.

I do not know what his policy is on borrowing money at fixed interest. I suspect he rarely needs to.

There is a sophisticated and smashing variation of Drag the Word In, which as far as I know has no name. I first heard of it from Jeremy Bullmore, creative director of J. Walter Thompson, who may have invented it. Like Drag The Word In, it is best as a game for two players but any number can play. It is a two-part game.

The first part might be called Invent the Proverb. This is the difficult bit. The task is to invent a phrase which *sounds* like a proverb we have all known and loved from birth, a cliché tried and trusted and true—which must totally lack any meaning deeper than its face value. While *sounding* pregnant with oracular philosophic subtlety, the words must mean only what they say, neither a profound jot nor sapient tittle more.

Jeremy Bullmore's two best examples are:

'Someone has to bury the undertaker.' (Which cannot be denied.)
'It may not be the man who saws the logs who needs the fire.' (Which he feels has perhaps too Russian a flavour to qualify in an Anglo-Saxon game.)

An example which at first sight seems perfect, but on further examination fails to qualify on the grounds of possible inherent profundity is:

'Only a young doctor has never lost a patient.' (And only a new agency has never lost a client.)

Terry Clark, the marketing director of Coty, invented:

'The face that laughs is also the face that cries.'

And my own favourite, which nobody else much likes, is:

'Only a foolish watchmaker is deaf to the Music of Time.'

To return to the game. Once the proverbs have been invented and agreed as being satisfactory, the second part of the game is to use them in a meeting, just as in Drag The Word In. They must be spoken seriously, preferably pompously, and they must sound like a relevant and thoughtful contribution to the subject under discussion. The first person to use his proverb in this way wins. If anyone in the room shows even the slightest awareness that something a trifle odd has been said, the player is deemed disqualified.

Practical jokes are normally the creative department's department. All admen enjoy a jolly jape now and again. The more juvenile the better. At Sharps the boardroom drink cupboard, like most boardroom drink cupboards, had a lock on it. Only directors were supposed to have keys, but everyone seemed to. Norman Griffiths had the lock changed. Somehow, within days everyone had the new keys. He changed the lock again.

To help Norman, the creative department acquired a Great Dane which it stationed by the drink cupboard in the boardroom. Then it built a massive cardboard padlock, about four foot high, and locked his office with it.

A good game to learn early on in your advertising career, when you are still comparatively young and impoverished, is Feed Me. I learnt this one from an art director who was an especially fine player, though—for obvious reasons—girls are generally better at this game than men.

'If you ever want dinner at the Mirabelle,' the art director said, 'just convince Oliver Knox that he's hurt your feelings. Make a fuss when he turns down one of your ideas. Pretend to be deeply wounded. Look baleful, even *maimed*. It always works.'

It does.

It is very dangerous for an agency to indulge in competitive sports against its own clients. The idea is always a tempting one. A happy day at the golf club or on the cricket pitch, followed by a few convivial hours at the bar, followed by dinner, followed by a grateful letter from a closer, friendlier client. What better way could there be to cement a healthy client/agency relationship? Agencies and clients who play together might reasonably be expected to stay together.

But beware. The way to the green is mined with multitudinous dangers. The first, and most important, is the little difficulty about winning or losing. If by chance you or your team are greatly superior to the poor client at your chosen sport, and thrash him soundly, he is hardly likely to love you for it. If in this situation you deliberately contrive to play badly, almost certainly he will notice and love you still less.

If on the other hand your client turns out to be a semi-pro who once got a trial cap for England, and trounces you without effort, your status in his eyes is unlikely to be enhanced. I once played chess with Tim Ambler, marketing director of International Distillers and Vintners home trade, after having spent the afternoon with him watching the Oxford v Cambridge varsity rugger match. (That's my kind of sport: watching, I mean.) By the evening I was tired and mildly sozzled. I played appallingly. I wasted moves, missed opportunities, threw away my queen, and lost ignominiously. For some days I was depressed by the certainty that no intelligent client could possibly entrust an advertising budget of some hundreds of thousands of pounds to anyone who played chess not merely so badly, but so totally feeble-mindedly.

It is often suggested that the correct way to solve the win or lose dilemma is to allow the client to win narrowly after a long hard match. This is fine, but presumes you are in full control of the situation and that the client is in league with your plan. Which is rarely the case.

In competitive team games another major area of risk is the team. Few agencies are large enough to sport a team composed entirely of account executives. Anyway most agencies succumb to the desire to put on to the field the best team possible. This invariably means playing a few messenger boys, or production assistants, or traffic trainees—all of whom are almost bound to be fitter than pub-crawling copywriters or expensively-lunched account executives. Unfortunately these lads tend not always to understand that it is sometimes better to lose battles in order to win wars; nor in the bar afterwards are they always quite statesmanlike in their criticisms of the client's intelligence and the agency's efficiency.

The final hazard is that it is often unwise for agencies and clients to become too thick socially. Many clients prefer to keep their agency relationships simple, clean and businesslike. They do not want to give business to an agency because they like drinking with them; they want to give business to their agency because it is good at advertising. The two things are not incompatible of course. It is quite possible for clients to like the people who produce excellent work for them. But too much socializing arouses clients' guilt feelings. And too much time spent on the playing field may seduce an agency into forgetting that it is their advertising, and not their eye for a ball, that counts.

10 Name Games

Names are a bane of agency life. Following fairly common agency practice, when Foote, Cone and Belding, New York, were working on the launch of a new Ford in 1955 they organized a competition among their employees in New York, London and Chicago. The prize for whoever thought of the finally-chosen name for the car was to be one of the brand-new motors.

In less than no time Foote, Cone and Belding had received eighteen thousand names including Zoom, Zip, Benson, Henry and Drof (try spelling it backwards). Suspecting that Fords might regard this list as a trifle unwieldy, FCB cut it down to a mere six thousand possibles.

'There you are,' an FCB man said triumphantly flopping a sheaf of papers on to the table at the presentation to Ford, 'six thousand names, all alphabetized and cross-referenced.'

'But,' the Ford man gasped, 'we don't want six thousand names. We only want one.'

The situation was then critical because the making of dies for the new car was about to begin. FCB cancelled all leaves in their New York and Chicago offices and instituted a crash programme to cut down the list of six thousand to ten in three days, including a weekend. Before the weekend was over four names—Corsair, Citation, Pacer and Ranger—had emerged as favourites, with Corsair head and shoulders above the rest.

'Along with other factors in its favour,' a Ford executive stated, 'it had done splendidly in the sidewalk interviews. The free associations with Corsair were rather romantic— pirate, swashbuckler, things like that. For its opposite we got "princess" or something else attractive of that order. Just what we wanted.'

The short list of names was presented to Edward R. Breech, Ford's chairman. He did not like any of them.

'Let's call it Edsel,' he said, naming it after Henry Ford II's father, the only son of founder Henry, and president of the Ford Motor Company from 1918 until his death in 1943.

They did.*

What, one might ask, precisely is a brand name? What do we mean by Omo? Or Persil or Kelloggs or Heinz? Does the concept of Guinness function in exactly the same way as the concept of Boots the Chemist? And why do Boots frequently invent separate brand names for the goods they manufacture and sell—e.g. Strepsils, or No. 7 Cosmetics—instead of simply calling them Boots' lozenges and Boots' Cosmetics?

The brand name is an interesting middle territory between the naming of individuals and the naming of things. We all know that we call Thomas Herbert Wilberforce by the name Thomas Herbert Wilberforce because it would be confusing and non-functional to call him and everyone else A Person. We remember how inconvenient it was at school when there were two Thomas Herbert Wilberforces in the class (those terrible fights over school caps). And we know that many big organizations use numbers instead of names, however degrading it may be for the individuals involved, partly to ensure that Thomas Herbert Wilberforce doesn't get fired or sent to the glasshouse—when it should have been Thomas Herbert Wilberforce all along.

Equally we know that such an elaborate system of differentiation is not normally necessary for things. Every table, every pencil, every salt cellar in the house does not need an individual name. In conversations we say 'Pass me that pencil' or 'I saw a pencil'; and if there is any doubt in the mind of the listener which object is being referred to, the addition of a simple differentiating adjective almost always suffices to make the meaning clear.

---

* From *The Fate of the Edsel*, a marvellously illuminating book about business by John Brooks. Gollancz, 1963.

The underlying reasons why humans have particular names, in all societies, whereas things almost never do are many and complex. (And of course it is interesting and significant when things *are* given particular, individual names.) To understand how advertising works it is vital to understand how brand names work, in between human names and thing names, and the way businessmen make them work.

Historically, of course, a brand name was usually the name of the individual who made the goods: Pear's Soap, Wedgwood's Pottery. The individual marked his name on the products he manufactured as a farmer brands his cattle. But not for the same reason. The farmer branding his cattle was seeking to prove ownership, the manufacturer was not. He was seeking, as economists regularly point out, to stop people using the general noun 'pottery' and start them using the particular name Wedgwood.

The reasons for a manufacturer wishing to do this are now fairly obvious, though they probably were not always. It makes it easier for a customer to recognize and re-purchase the manufacturer's products and to recommend them to others (manufacturers always think their products are wonderful). On the other hand, it also makes it easier for an individual to recognize and *not* re-purchase and to warn others off those products. Thus from the start the concept of the brand name was closely interrelated with the much vaguer concept of quality.

Professor John Wisdom has argued that all nouns are predictive. Brand names are more than predictive, they are promissory. They are promises from the manufacturer of a product to the person who buys and uses it. If a brand name fails to keep its promises over any length of time, it slowly loses its meaning. And its promises are both many and specific. Having experienced a bar of Pear's Soap once, I wish to be certain that when I next buy something called Pear's Soap I obtain a product entirely similar to the first. It must be precisely similar in *all* aspects: appearance, touch, smell, consistency, even, if needs be, taste. (Who's to know how many clumsy bathers get soap in their mouths when they're washing their faces?) And any sensible manufacturer who wishes to stay in business will control his production to ensure that I am not disappointed. If he changes any ingredient or aspect of his product he will do so with care and trepidation, praying that I will not notice. Unless, of course, he deliberately wants me to notice, in which case he will mark his product 'New, Improved' (and he will then pray that I agree with him).

This completeness of specification, which a brand name promises, is an area where its between-noun-and-name function is clearest. Soap comes in many forms, and there may even be arguments about whether certain things which function (or maybe taste) like soap really are soap or not. Individuals come in only one form (by definition). There is only one Ludwig Wittgenstein, concrete, finite and specific. And there is only one Daz—even though there are any number of packets of it. Another soap powder, even one chemically the same as Daz but coming in a packet named Fuzz, would not be Daz—just as an individual who thought and acted like Wittgenstein but looked like Winston Churchill could not be Wittgenstein. The appearance and packaging are an intrinsic part of the total. This is not normally true of the generic 'soap'. An individual's name refers to something unique; a noun refers to innumerable similar things; a brand name refers to innumerable things which are uniquely similar.

Clients suffer terrible neuroses about brand names. For Player's we kept a list of several thousand possible new cigarette names always at the ready. All of them had been cleared by the lawyers, many of them had been researched and re-researched. One favourite which the agency regularly recommended and which Player's regularly rejected was Buckingham. Geoffrey Kent, then Marketing and Sales Director at Player's, was convinced that on the hoardings Buckingham's initial letter would suffer grievous defacement at the hands of small boys throughout the country. Finally Rothman's launched Buckingham. It has not been much of a success, but I did not see a single defaced B.

When at MCR we were launching a home-brewed beer for IDV we undertook the most daunting naming task of all, inventing a human person's name for the brand. Agreeing a child's name with your spouse can bring strife and tears. Imagine then having to agree a fictitious new name like Mary Baker or Betty Crocker within the agency and then with the whole of a client's marketing department. The telephone directory was our oyster.

It had been agreed that the name should sound very Anglo-Saxon-traditional, redolent of the true country flavour of olde Englishe countrie beere. Our first lists predictably ran into hundreds. Unable to cancel everybody's leave in our New York and Chicago offices, I simply whistled through the sheets myself and selected a short list of ten:

Tom Armstrong	Edwin Wright
Ben Fielding	Adam Knight
Bill Buckley	Matthew Palmer
Tom Caxton	James Proctor
John Holbrook	Will Thorpe

I sent them to Roger Booth, managing director of the IDV subsidiary in charge of the home-brewed beer project, telling him that he could perm any christian/surname combination that he cared to from amongst them. Being a sensible chap he passed the list straight to Jasper Grinling, then IDV's Group Managing Director, and asked him to pick his choice the following weekend. Once Jasper had decided, that would settle the matter.

On Monday morning my telephone rang.

'Winston.' It was Jasper. 'I simply wasted all of Sunday afternoon on this little problem of yours. And I've had a few ideas myself.... Now what do you think of these?' Within five minutes he had suggested a further dozen or so possible alternatives. 'Up to you entirely of course,' he said; 'you're the expert. It's your decision.' I put down the telephone despondently. Instead of choosing one name from the original ten, we now had a list of more than twenty again. I telephoned Roger Booth and explained.

Fortunately Roger is a more decisive fellow than I. 'Did Jasper say there were any on your list he particularly disliked?' he asked.

'Well, no.'

'Which of them do you like best?'

'I don't know. Tom Caxton I think.'

'OK. Tom Caxton it is, then. Jasper said it was up to you. So you chose it for him, by proxy. Tom Caxton. I like it. I knew Jasper would pick the right one.'

Returning now to Mr. Pear, the situation is comparatively simple so long as he sticks to his last and keeps on making soap. But what happens when he irritatingly starts to manufacture toothbrushes? Pear's Toothbrushes he calls them. What is he saying? What does he wish me to understand? More importantly, what *do* I understand?

Clearly Mr. Pear is making a very general statement about his new toothbrushes. He is saying: 'You know that soap which you like so much. I make it. So if I make a toothbrush you'll like that too. Trust me.' And, surprisingly or not (that is another question), people will trust him. Thus at this point the name ceases to function as a *brand* name, becoming instead, in accurate jargon, a *manufacturer's* name. It is now, if you like, as much a description of the manufacturer as of the product. Alf Pear, he's honest, trustworthy and reliable; know him, know his products—they are an extension of himself, that is why they have his name. In some senses old Alf Pear was associating his personality with his soap, via his name, right from the beginning. But the function was not so clear then. Or to put it another way: he may well, in naming the soap, have been consciously saying 'This is of me'—but his listeners (purchasers) understood the name in a different way, taking it initially to be simply a name for a subdivision of the product category soap.

Now what happens when a manufacturer invents a meaningless word to describe his product, instead of giving it his own name? Omo or Surf or Persil, instead of Lord Leverhulme's patent powders? There is clearly no suggestion of a human being guaranteeing the quality of the product by bestowing upon it his name. These words come to have a meaning, partly created by the product itself, partly created by the product's packaging, partly by its advertising, partly by the kind of people who use it and by what they say about it.

The curious thing is that having invented the word, and having launched it into the world, the manufacturer largely ceases to have control of its precise meaning. Like any other word, it takes on shades of different meanings to different people; it acquires overtones and associations. For example, the brand name Fairy has overtones of mildness and gentleness; any new Fairy product will be thought to have those qualities. And the meanings of brand names change all the time. Senior Service used to imply mildness, youth and femininity; now it implies strength, old-fashionedness and masculinity. As with Tom Caxton, every brand name is chosen initially because it sounds and feels right for the brand, in the hope that it conveys the desired subtleties of meaning; once launched, the name is literally in the public domain.

To discover what their brand names 'mean', manufacturers spend small fortunes on market research each year, asking the public. This work represents an exceptionally sophisticated and advanced form of linguistic analysis. No lexicographer can afford it, many would not think it a proper thing to do. But manufacturers with millions of pounds invested in their brand names—some years ago Kimberley-Clark put a value of £10,000,000 on the word Kleenex, and at that price it was probably going cheap—have developed specific techniques for getting people to define what brand names mean to them. This research gives manufacturers what is commonly called 'the brand image'. It defines, sometimes mathematically, the halo of meanings and connotations surrounding any particular brand name. (All brands have images, of course, whether any market research is carried out or not. Research merely helps manufacturers to understand and specify accurately what that image is.)

The simplest research technique is the group discussion, which merely brings eight or nine people together into a room where they discuss at length, for perhaps an hour or more, a particular brand or brands. All their thoughts about the brand, all that the brand name means to them, quickly become apparent. A more sophisticated technique asks people to position brand names on, say, relevant seven point scales. (Establishing which scales are relevant to any particular brand is a separate technique in itself.) At each end of each scale are pairs of opposites, and the exact position in which people place the brand name between these opposites gives a mathematical definition of its 'meaning'. For example, relevant scales for beer might be: strong/weak; bitter/sweet; rough/smooth; light/heavy; drunk mainly by women/drunk mainly by men; drunk mainly by the young/drunk mainly by the old; good for you/not good for you: and Guinness would be rated differently on each of these scales from Double Diamond from Worthington from Watney's Red. The way each would be rated would depend, as mentioned earlier, partly on the beer itself, partly on its advertising and so on. All of which together define the total meaning of the brand name and its 'image'. (Though since the number of scales which can be applied is limited, and I believe the connotations adhering to any word to be infinite, only the most important meanings can be measured.)

To return to an earlier question, it is as a result of considering the *total* meaning of a brand or manufacturer's name that Boots chose to call their cosmetic products No. 7 Cosmetics rather than simply Boots' Cosmetics. Whether with the benefit of market research, or whether on the basis of hunch and judgement, Boots apparently decided that their company name has overtones of drugs (medicinal rather than hallucinatory), seriousness, authority, perhaps dreariness and conservatism. Cosmetics, on the other hand, need to be glamorous, young, light-hearted and attractive. In these circumstances to transfer the overtones of 'Boots' directly to their cosmetic products would be to ensure that women did not buy them. Cosmetics, even more than most other goods, need to satisfy psychological as well as functional needs. In practice, Boots have tried to get the best of both worlds. The brand name of the product range is No. 7 Cosmetics—goodness knows why No. 7; perhaps a superstitious executive thought it would convey good luck to girls using the products and thus be a lucky number for him. But they have also made clear, which they did not have to, that the range is in fact made by Boots. They are, in other words, trying to add Boots' manufacturer's (or in this case retailer's) image, that of a purveyor of generally reliable and good quality products, to the cosmetics' brand image of glamour and excitement. And they will eventually be able to discover whether or not they are achieving the communication of this rather complicated message by researching the meaning of the brand name 'No. 7 Cosmetics'.

Until now I have implied that brand names and manufacturers' names are wholly separate concepts and are seen to be so. This is of course not the case. Tom Caxton is really a brand name disguised as a manufacturer's name. Another example of the overlap and confusion between the two is Player's. John Player and Sons have always made cigarettes and tobaccos: lots of different kinds with lots of different brand names but all under the John Player manufacturer's name, with its general reputation for quality. Over the years, the sales of one of their products, brand name Medium Navy Cut cigarettes, raced ahead of the others. This brand eventually came to dominate the public consciousness of Player's products. Slowly Player's came to mean not only the manufacturer, but also the brand. If, in the 1950's you asked a tobacconist for 'twenty Players', you were given twenty Medium Navy Cut cigarettes. The fact that Player's also made Weights Cigarettes, Bachelor Cigarettes and a host of cigars and tobaccos—and that everybody knew Player's made those products—was irrelevant. 'Players' meant 'Medium Navy Cut'.

Unfortunately for John Player & Sons, in the late 1950's smoking fashions changed. Non-filter cigarettes, for health and cost reasons, began to be smoked less and less. And the name Player's—who as a company had all along produced filter-tipped cigarettes—came to convey hot, strong, old-fashioned, non-filter cigarettes. Throughout the late 1950's and early 1960's the company's fortunes suffered badly, and although they brought out many new brands during this period, the overtones of the name Player's were detrimental to them all.

This is, after all, not illogical. It is the way all other words work. The word 'red' means certain generalized perceptions to us; if someone uses the word 'red', these perceptions are defined; if he wanted us to think of blue, but was forced to keep using the word 'red', he would be unlikely to succeed in communicating with us. *Until* by repetition and demon-stration he taught us that red now *meant* blue.

And that is very roughly what Player's did. By bringing out new filter cigarettes, with new names—and advertising them heavily—they slowly changed the public's conception of the word Player's. By calling their successive brands Play-er's Gold Leaf, Player's No. 6, Player's No. 10, JPS and most recently John Player's Carlton, they have moved Players back to being a manufacturer's name, a guarantee of quality and reliability. (Established quality and reliability being par-ticularly important in the cigarette market.) There is still some slight rub-off from the old Player's Medium Navy Cut. Player's new brands are still seen as slightly stronger than some of their competitors, but this is quickly fading.

Wines illustrate another aspect of brand naming. The French *Appellation Contrôlée* system is, of course, a system of branding, of saying wines with this or that name on them will be of a particular style and quality, reliable and consis-tent (theoretically) from bottle to bottle. The cognoscenti realize that the 'brands' are place names where the grapes were grown. However the situation is confused by Château names and shippers' names, which have varying functions. Market research shows clearly that novitiates to wine confuse Beaujolais with Louis Latour. And the shippers' marketing of genuine brands in the traditional soap-bar sense (such as Mateus, Justina, Don Cortez, Nicolas and others) confuses the situation still further. What does Mateus mean? Does it mean that the wine always comes from the same place? No, it doesn't. Then can it mean that the wine consistently tastes the same? No, it cannot, quite, though the wine makers try hard. Charrington Vintners, who market a pleasant enough cheap brand called Hirondelle have come out into the open. We will buy wine, for Hirondelle they say, from anywhere; from Austria or Algeria or Patagonia if needs be: so long as we offer a consistent quality (that word again).

But what is quality when applied to a wine? Indefinable.

Which is why the French set about solving the problem from the other end, guaranteeing (well, trying to) the wine by branding its source. On the other hand, we may, philosophically at least, wonder whether a wine that is labelled Beaujolais, tastes like Beaujolais, is chemically exactly like Beaujolais but was grown in Paraguay, is meaningfully fraudulent.

It is quite important for ad makers to understand the rather special ways in which brand names function. Falling halfway between nouns and proper names, they are a peculiar breed of word. The group of words which function most similarly to brand names are, I believe, to be found in botany. Names of flowers and plants—significantly, often again the names of individuals—are equally promissory and each is specific while referring to an infinite number of individual entities. They say that a rose is a rose is a rose; but what if it's an Ena Harkness?

11 The Marketing Revolution Cometh Again

It seems astonishing, but there are still books being published, articles being written, and speeches being made announcing the coming of the marketing revolution. In turn, each prophet of this impending millennium warns production oriented companies that they must take heed of the needs and desires of their customers, or perish. New ideas take a while to catch on of course, but this one was commonplace sixty years ago. In 1914 two of advertising's great champions, E. S. Hole and John Hart* wrote:

> We so often see old firms of standing and repute, equipped with a staff of experts who have grown grey in the accumulation of technical experience and efficiency in product only, go down like ninepins before a rival whose special abilities are directed towards efficient selling.... After many centuries of trading, and after blinking the fact to the very last ditch, it has finally become clear to the manufacturer that the imperious consumer can be evaded no longer and that he is and will always remain, the final arbiter in the warfare of commerce.

The new marketing revolution has nothing to do with the age-old dichotomy between production-oriented companies and sales-oriented companies. There can be few companies still in business which do not at least pay lip service to the cliché that the customer is always right. The marketing revolution that cometh is consumerism.

Advertising and consumerism are traditionally antagonistic to each other. The extreme position is taken by the

---
* 'Advertising and Progress' by E. S. Hole and John Hart. Published in Review of Reviews, 1914.

British Labour Party's 1972 Green Paper on Advertising. This recommends that 50 per cent of all advertising expenditure be taxed, and that the Government should spend the money so raised on a National Consumer Authority—an independent agency 'empowered to survey all consumer matters, (or to sponsor tests of) claims made by advertisers, and effectively to publicize the results of its own and all other relevant work'.

To carry out the programme effectively, the Green Paper rightly predicts, would cost many millions of pounds each year. Before making this recommendation the Green Paper notes with surprise, as many others have noted with surprise before it, that despite the apparently irrefutable strength of consumerists' arguments, consumerism as a powerful mass-movement has continuously failed to get started. Nearly half a century after Stuart Chase published his influential best seller, *Your Money's Worth*, in 1927, the Consumer Union in the United States boasts only 1.3 million members—less than 1 per cent of the population. In the United Kingdom, fifteen years after the publication of the first issue of *Which?* in 1957, the Consumer Association has only 600,000 members —just over 1 per cent of the population. It is indeed difficult to refute the opinions of the Molony Committee on Consumer Protection in 1962:

> ...it is difficult to avoid the conclusion that the consumer does not think she, or he, is ill-served ... there was no cogent evidence of consumer dissatisfaction.

A view echoed repeatedly by leading consumerists throughout the world. In 1966 Eirlys Roberts of *Which?* confirmed the picture: 'It is not possible to say that consumer reports have any large, direct influence....' And Ralph Nader is not surprisingly dissatisfied: 'Very little progress really. It's a push and shove situation.' In Sweden, where consumerist legislation has gone furthest, the results have been confused and unsatisfactory. Why has the much-heralded consumer-protection movement made so little progress? The standard answer, given for example in the Labour Party's Green Paper, is lack of money. Compared to the wealth of advertising and business, the consumerists' financial resources are pitifully tiny. But inadequate funds have never stopped a movement with fundamental emotional appeal. The nineteenth-century Trade Unionists, supported only by the impoverished working class, confronted profit-hungry big business far more successfully than have their twentieth-century affluent middle-class consumerist counterparts. Nevertheless, particularly in the USA, the influence of consumerists steadily grows stronger.

Advertising exists to sell goods and services. Some people feel strongly that it should not be necessary to *sell* things: produce a better mousetrap and the world will beat a pathway to your door and all that. In practice, as even the kibbutzim and the communist countries have found, it is impossible to co-ordinate production and demand exactly. Selling and price are the buffers between. When demand exceeds production selling is unnecessary; when production exceeds demand you have no choice but to sell—or waste.

Advertising, the mass-selling of popular goods and services, performs several useful functions here. It helps manufacturers stabilize and predict their production schedules; it informs consumers about the products available and goes a long way to guarantee their quality.

Nobody claims that the production of goods and services is the most admirable of all human activities. Certainly nobody has ever been so daft as to claim that all the good things in life are solely to be found in advertisements. Advertising affects only a small part of our lives. There is virtually no advertising concerned with law and order, public health, income tax, education, country rambles, science or the arts. Advertising is a small industry, with less than 16,000 people employed in agencies, about as many as work in one medium-sized industrial company, and with only about £60 million a year spent on the production and placing of advertisements. Most areas of our lives are in no way affected by advertising. Yet it is surely foolish to argue that those areas where advertising is involved—cars, cosmetics, chocolate, clothes—give no pleasure or are totally unimportant.

Man's relationship with material objects is an extremely complex one. From the start anthropoids chipped away at their flints ever-anxious to make a better *coup de poing*. Watch a baby, just a few months old, grab at objects it likes the look or feel of. Try to take away the scrap of paper or old sock upon which it has temporarily become fixated and you will suffer screams of righteous fury not dissimilar from those I make myself when I cannot have a car or painting that I have set my heart upon. Experimental psychologists have shown that babies react quite differently to people and to things—and gain great pleasure from both. Anthropologists, seeking a way to distinguish man from other animals defined him as a tool-making animal. Not a thinking or speaking or a cello-playing animal. Materialism—the involvement of human beings with material objects—is part of us. Advertising is its most obvious and most public manifestation.

One of the best marketing men I ever met sold me an Alfa-Romeo. Immediately I began the test-drive I knew that I wanted the car. As we sped smoothly through the streets I was totally seduced, blinded by temporary passion, unable to find a single fault in the beautiful Italian chariot. Enraptured, I eulogized the gears, the driving position, the acceleration, the purr of the engine. I delivered a brief but emotional encomium on the width of the rear-view mirror.

Suddenly I remembered that I should be playing hard to get, simulating lack of interest so that I could get the highest possible trade-in price for my rattling old Ford Consul. Desperately I searched for some imperfection which I could castigate with suitable venom. Eventually I found one.

'Why,' I asked furiously, 'is there no cigarette lighter in this car? Even my old Ford has a cigarette lighter.'

The salesman sitting beside me was unshaken. 'Alfa Romeo,' he answered, 'make motor cars. If you need a cigarette lighter, I suggest you contact the Ronson company.'

That's good marketing: deciding what is relevant in a product and what is not. More precisely, deciding what your customers will find relevant—and then promoting it hard.

That is what is meant by getting the creative strategy right. It is often very difficult.

Why do people buy the things they do? Like many other apparently naïve questions, this one has no quick and simple answer. Why will a woman buy a hat rather than a bottle of whisky or eight pounds of milk chocolate? Why will a man spend an annual fortune on one brand of cigarettes rather than another, and rather than an altogether healthier set of dumb-bells? Almost unconsciously we incessantly make tiny decisions, choosing between what we want most and what we are prepared to do without.

Without subscribing to solipsism or to the more eccentric views of Bishop Berkeley, it is accurate to say that people do not buy things. They buy satisfactions, both subjective and objective, that those things are going to deliver to them personally. And before they buy, they unconsciously assess the differing satisfactions that different products will provide, and simultaneously balance this against the alternative satisfactions of not spending their money at all. Watch a child in a toy shop, wondering whether to buy this or that or to save his pocket money until next week. It's the archetypal purchasing-decision process.

In order to help us make these decisions as wisely as possible, to choose the products that will bring us most satisfactions for our money, we need to know as much as possible about the products. This is what consumerists and, indeed, ordinary members of the public in market research demand from advertising: never mind the glamour and the sell, they say, just give us all the facts.

But this demand, like many other apparently simple and straightforward requests, just cannot be met. As a simple example let's take detergents—a product-field which draws much critical fire. The facts about a detergent could include, both for itself and in comparison with other detergents:

(1) Its chemical formula.
(2) Its price and price per ounce.

(3) Its packaging, both material and surface design.

(4) Its effectiveness in washing different types of material.

(5) Its effectiveness in different washing situations.

(6) Its effectiveness with different hardnesses of water.

(7) Its smell.

(8) Its danger if eaten by children, or as a pollutant.

(9) Its name.

(10) How long it has been on the market.

(11) Where it can/can't be bought.

(12) The profit the retailer/wholesaler/manufacturer makes out of it.

(13) How many people are employed in making it.

(14) Whether the raw materials are indigenous or imported.

(15) How many people use it, and which people they are.

(16) What the names of the people are who work on the advertising.

(17) Whether the manufacturer practises racial/religious/anti-female prejudice.

...and so on. They are all facts about the detergent, important to different people at different times. It is easy to imagine Germaine Greer rallying housewives to spurn Omo if she discovered that Unilever disapproved of Women's Lib. But could all these facts go into each advertisement?

There is no such thing as the complete or whole truth about any product. The mechanics' manual tells you only *part* of the truth about a motor car; the chemical formula will tell you almost nothing about a lipstick or a shirt. The fundamental job of advertising is to distil and communicate, pithily and economically, those facts about any product which will be most meaningful, most interesting and most relevant to consumers—and therefore will be most likely to persuade them to buy. This is what the endless advertising arguments over product positioning and brand image and creative strategy are all about. Communicating relevantly, as every competent copywriter instinctively knows, is the essence of effective advertising. It is also the essence of effective consumerism. Consumerist reports don't give *all* the facts about products either. They give the facts that consumerists consider relevant, meaningful, and interesting. And on the evidence of the majority of housewives voting with their purses, the advertisers still seem a lot better than the consumerists at assessing just which facts are relevant, meaningful and interesting to their customers.

Because, and this again is a point that consumerists have failed to grasp, advertisers understand that products are not merely the sum of their molecules. As well as being functional, objective entities, the products they make and we buy also arouse subjective, emotional reactions; and these feelings can be every bit as important as the measurable mechanical criteria. If we were all sensible, value-conscious economic beings we would not smoke, eat chocolates, drive too fast, drink too much, gamble, waste time and money on works of art or buy expensive fancy clothes. The thrill of buying a new motor car is only tangentially related to its consumption in miles per gallon. There is a glamour and excitement in products that is very real and pleasurable for most people. Advertising enhances and increases the glamour, the excitement and the pleasure. That is why it works. We wish to feel good about the products we buy and use; so we buy and use products advertising has made us feel good about.

There is no way in which advertising can tell the *whole* truth. Indeed the concept of a *whole* truth would not be very acceptable to a philosopher or an artist, even though it may be moderately useful in a court of law.

People love products. Advertising, as super-salesman, tries to give them the relevant facts while making the products seem as nice as possible. Sometimes the salesman oversells his goods, jams his foot in the door too irritatingly, neglects to make clear that his medicines won't cure every ill. Noticing the few rotten branches, advertising's enemies wish to chop down the whole tree.

The fundamental reason for the relative ineffectuality of consumerism to date is that it does not, and cannot, satisfactorily take account of people's emotional involvement with the products they buy. Consumer tests only work well for functional products—mechanical goods with easily definable uses whose efficiency can be measured, preferably mathematically. That is why cars and consumer durables have borne the brunt of consumerists' attacks. It is comparatively easy to measure whether one dishwasher is more efficient than another. How do you judge whether one tie is 'better' than another? How do you quantitatively measure different wines or books or fabric designs or chocolates? Or handbags or furniture or beer? If personal taste is a major component in the purchasing decision, arithmetical calculations of abstract value become unimportant.

For functional products too, personal taste can be all-important. I certainly have never chosen a car for purely sensible, cost/value reasons. This is not to argue that the consumerist information on mechanical durables is worthless. It is very useful. It is desirable to have as much relevant information as possible to help us decide which products will give us most satisfactions for our money. The consumerist information is often simply not the *most* relevant information. The public is not much interested in the nutritional value of breakfast cereals or the exact weight of meat in canned stews. If these aspects of the products were of vital importance to consumers, manufacturers would quickly react by making (and advertising) more nutritional and more meaty brands. There is no reason to believe that Kelloggs are violently prejudiced against nutritional cereals, if these are what the public really want. Indeed in the USA, after forty breakfast cereals were castigated by leading consumerist Robert Choate for being low in nutritional value, the manufacturers added specific nutrients to twenty-six of them.

The most relevant information about products is that which the advertisers, if they are doing their job properly, will be trying to give. It is usually extremely difficult to know what aspects of a product are the most relevant to most consumers. Consumerists rush headlong into this basic difficulty. The relevant information may be factual, it may be emotional. Consumerists concentrate exclusively on the hard, functional facts; perhaps advertisers concentrate too much on soft, emotional persuasion. That is why advertising and consumerism are now mutually antagonistic; they need not be. They should be complementary.

Manufacturers have no innate prejudice against producing 'better' products—if these are what most people want and are prepared to pay for. The very concept of brand names is inextricably intertwined with the concept of quality, as I hope was shown in the last chapter. Advertisers have no inborn prejudice against producing factual, detailed ads—if these are what most people want and are prepared to read. But experience proves that more people will buy imperfect Fords than perfect Ferraris; and more people will read the sensational *Daily Mirror* than the serious and informative *Times*.

Most large manufacturers are not devious blackguards trying to rob and cheat their unwary customers. They are made up of mere executives, more or less adequate at their jobs, trying to balance the three-way conflicting demands of their employees for greater salaries, their shareholders for greater profits, and their customers for better value. By banging the consumerist drum fiercely and frighteningly, the militants are ensuring that the customers' demands—which had perhaps been a little too quiet over the years—are now being heard.

Consumerists are, in reality, helping the marketing process. They are, cantankerously, bringing to manufacturers' attention desirable product-improvements. (It's cheaper than market research.) That consumerism has grown to its present importance points an accusatory finger at modern marketing, and highlights areas of inadequate sensitivity. If manufacturers co-operated generously with consumerists, and if consumerists tried to appreciate the emotional role that products play in people's lives, we would all be helping the imperious consumer to enjoy his life a little more. Which would be a tiny marketing revolution.

12 *No Facts Are Better than Most*

Watching the market research industry grow up is like being in at the evolution of a new species. The evolutionary tree is growing many branches, some of which are useful and are beginning to function quite well, others of which will atrophy and vanish. The fully developed beast will one day be extremely powerful. Today it is still in a stage of primitive development.

A few years ago, market research reports were always late, and were replete with inaccuracies. It was unwise to draw up a Critical Path Analysis which relied on the market research arriving on time, it was foolhardy to trust to any figures you yourself had not carefully checked.

Nowadays market research is more or less efficient. Reports occasionally arrive ahead of time. Percentages add up to 100, give or take a few points; management summaries are literate, or at least coherent; research managers rarely need to write those miserable memos explaining away questions which have not been asked, samples which have fallen short, unfathomable computer tables which have been printed by an idiot, signifying nothing. Today the machinery works adequately, bleeping and buzzing a little when strained. Today the problems facing the market-research industry are intellectual and financial. The fundamental problem is financial. Market research is an economical way of obtaining data which could always be obtained more accurately at greater cost. A referendum or general election is necessarily more accurate than an opinion poll of voting intentions; it is also more time-consuming and far more expensive. Obtaining a register of the names and addresses of every individual who bought his products would give a manufacturer the opportunity to exert a great influence over them; if he could afford it.

Being by its nature something of a cheap-jack method of collecting data, market research has tied a noose and thrust its own head in it by selling itself and the data it provides too cheaply. As a result, too inaccurately. Market researchers meet this criticism by insisting that the work they do, like the work of physicists and chemists, results only in probabilities mathematically calculable and verifiable. If an opinion poll shows the Conservatives leading by, say, 2 per cent then this means that the odds are 20 to 1 (or whatever) that in reality the Conservatives are leading by between 1.5 per cent and 2.5 per cent. Statistically true, but in practice irrelevant.

In practice, samples are never statistically perfect. In practice, the precise form of words each question asks will influence the results, and tiny changes of wording will produce changes in respondents' answers. In practice, probabilities only approximate to being reliable for total samples, and not for sub-groups.

Perhaps the worst offenders are the Shop Audit sales research companies. These claim, truthfully, that their total UK sample of, say, grocers is based on the most accurate Government data available. They also claim, with suitable humility, that their sales information usually correlates pretty well with Government production indices. Companies which buy Shop Audit data (and that includes just about every major consumer product marketing company around) treat each bi-monthly presentation as a new visitation by Moses down from Sinai. Sales managers are castigated because distribution has fallen in Scotland; brand managers win extra generous annual salary increments when their brand's market share puts on a few percentage points; ad agencies feel edgy when consumer sales lag behind retailers' purchases. The Shop Audit presenter preaches, and all are humbled; to dispute his data is tantamount to sacrilege. The simple fact is that total national, annual Shop Audit sales figures—the only figures that can ever be checked against outside sources— are usually fairly accurate. But their bi-monthly figures for small areas of the country—which can virtually never be checked and which create their own reality—are inevitably based on far smaller samples. Yet these figures are constantly acted upon.

'Some data is better than no data'—the basis upon which most market research is carried out today—is an obvious fallacy. Dubious data is in theory neither better nor worse than no data. In practice having dubious data is always worse. It allows idle people to act thoughtlessly, foolish people to cling to nonsense-facts and to hinder everyone else by dogmatically repeating them like parrots.

The industrial revolution of the last twenty years has been the growth and success of the mammoth retail chains. Tesco, Boots, Marks and Spencer, Sainsbury, Mothercare and the rest: all with outstanding records of long-term profitable growth. None of them uses market research very much, if at all. This is partly because rapidly growing companies rarely feel the need for the self-analysis and navel-gazing that market research implies; partly because retailers obtain daily sales information which is both more relevant and more accurate than market research data (though admittedly their sales sheets provide a very incomplete picture of their trade); mostly it is because executives in well-run companies need no crutch to help them make the decisions they believe in—a role often played by market research elsewhere.

Christopher Collins, the owner and managing director of Goya, has doubled sales and turned disastrous running losses into massive profits in the five years since he took over the company. If a market research company sends him a promotional mailing shot he politely returns it with the scribbled message: 'This company does not do market research.'

The fact that Shop Audit sub-samples are often too small to be statistically reliable is, in one sense, not the research companies' fault at all. They would be delighted to audit more shops and thus obtain sounder data. But they would then be forced to increase their charges to clients. And they obviously judge that they are already charging the maximum that the market will bear. This is the way that market research is tying its own noose and thrusting its head in.

Take for example the ubiquitous group-discussion. Every research company in the country carries out for clients group discussions amongst seven or so housewives—or maybe when the money is flowing lavishly two group-discussions among fourteen or so housewives. The functions of group discussions are to help manufacturers discover and understand the particular language consumers use about their products, and to generate hypotheses for large-scale testing. In practice, major decisions are based on the results of group discussions which the researcher, in his more scrupulous moments, knows have not been justified. Researchers pay lip service to this, and every group-discussion report starts with a caveat about the size of the sample and the uncertainty of the results. Few take any notice. And every researcher knows that if he didn't carry out this kind of work, the guy up the street would. So who can afford scruples these hard times?

The danger in group discussions, and in most current market-research, is that they assume a homogeneity which is non-existent. Except for staple commodities—sugar, potatoes, eggs, milk and so on—the great majority of products are minority products. Even some surprising ones. Pet-foods, toothpastes, motor cars, children's products, slimming products are all used regularly by less than half of the population.

Turning from general product fields to individual brands, usages become even tinier, still more of a minority. In jargon terms, market segmentation—the desire of groups of individuals to use products slightly different from those used by other groups of individuals—makes even standard majority markets act as an aggregate of minority markets—toilet soaps, detergents, newspapers, cigarettes, booze and so on. Top people may read newspapers but they don't take *The Sun*.

Move a stage further, from the minorities who use individual major brands, like Persil and Embassy cigarettes, to the even tinier number of people who *switch* brands in any one month—and these are the people whom advertising and marketing efforts mainly seek to influence. The futility of most head-counting studies and group discussions now shows up with pellucid clarity. Most manufacturers would be happy with 10 per cent of any major market, yet in a group discussion of seven housewives the odds are high that all seven will reject any brand liked by only one housewife in ten; at best one of the seven may show some slight interest in it.

If, overnight, 200,000 people started to use a product they had not been using before, a product costing them a mere 10 p every fortnight, they would spend £500,000 on that product in a year. Enough to interest any profit-hungry manufacturer in the country; nobody turns up their nose at £500,000. Yet these 200,000 represent only 1 in 200 adults: i.e. 0.5 per cent. That's an asterisk on any computer sheet. No research is ever carried out sufficiently accurately to measure it. If that 0.5 per cent were 50 per cent wrong, the true figure might be 0.75 per cent which would represent sales of £750,000 a year. Another asterisk.

These points sound so naïve that they should not need to be stated. Yet I have seen literally scores of quantitative surveys, group discussions and motivational studies covering perfumes and partworks, cigarettes and spot cures, soaps and skin creams, unit trusts and table wines, magazines and fizzy drinks and cough cures—researches carried out by the most responsible and best market research companies—which have ignored or skated over the problems of identifying the relevant minorities.

Once again the problem is cost. Many, though regrettably by no means all, researchers know full well that most of the work they do skims over the surface of fundamental marketing problems, producing imprecise generalities where specific precision is needed. They would gladly produce more meticulous research, interviewing the really interested one out of 100 housewives instead of the uninterested ninety-nine. Researching the wrong people is not merely futile; it is likely to be positively misleading. To take a much-simplified example: if I'm not interested in fast cars but am asked to choose between two sports models I'll probably choose the slower one. Precisely the opposite of the one the true likely purchaser would choose. A foolishly simple example, of course; amazing how often exactly comparable mistakes are made. It is expensive to isolate the ideal sample. And market researchers charge what they judge is the maximum that the market will bear. It is myopic.

Bill Shlackman, the American founder and head of William Shlackman Limited, probably the leading UK research company specializing in psychological and motivational surveys, was once selling a research prospectus to Charles Broadhead, then deputy chairman at John Player. The prospectus was for a psychological study among smokers of king-size cigarettes, 200 depth interviews for £2,500.

'£2,500,' Charles Broadhead mused, 'for 200 interviews. That's an awful lot of money.'

Bill Shlackman scrutinized his customer carefully. 'I'll give you a hundred interviews for twelve-fifty,' he offered.

The bargain was struck on the spot.

None of these particular criticisms apply to the continuous surveys which supply much useful and usable data—the JICNARS readership survey, the AGB TV Ratings, the Television Consumer Audit, the Target Group Index and two or three others. These massive expensive surveys *are* carried out on a sufficiently large scale to give realistic and reasonably reliable data. The high cost is syndicated because no individual client would be prepared to foot the total bill. It is the myriad, quick, ad hoc surveys which are too cheap and are indefensible.

There are also some smaller, continuous syndicated surveys which are wholly unsatisfactory. Every market research company wants to run syndicated continuous surveys, rather than carry out ad hoc projects. Continuous surveys offer guaranteed income, an easy-to-schedule workload, constant involvement with clients and little mental effort. Ad hoc projects call for the reverse, on all four counts. Small wonder that continuous survey contracts seem so desirable.

In their quest to find hidden corners of commerce where syndicated continuous surveys might find a lucrative market, market research companies are offering some pretty curious projects. The worst thing about them is the sloppiness of the sample design—a fault also frequently to be found in industrial market research. If you add together the views of seven stockbrokers, six jobbers, five merchant bankers, four accountants, three pension fund managers, two actuaries, and one investment analyst, what do you get? A partridge in a pear tree perhaps, but certainly not a meaningful reflection of City financial opinion. Infant-school arithmetic taught us the dangers of adding unlike to unlike.

It is this lack of precision, this lack of attention to pertinent detail, which results in so much unused market research, so many weighty duplicated and spiral-bound reports gathering dust on marketing executives' bookshelves. Volumes and volumes are produced which marketing executives read and ponder and forget, frustrated and impotent at being unable to take action on the basis of such fascinating facts, such apparently useful information.

Market research is still in its infancy. It is changing quickly as it grows. One day it will be an extremely influential force, both in business and in politics. It offers the prospect of a kind of greater democracy, if it can be made to work more perfectly. Perhaps eventually every home will be on-line to a central computer so that each of us can express our free opinions about every important issue, letting Government and industry alike know what we think of them. Just now market research is in dire need of a little rigorous intellectual self-discipline, a little less salesmanship, and realistic charging procedures.

13   How to Succeed at Sales Conferences

'Now while we have all been here in this hall...' the sales manager was on the stage addressing his troops at the end of the Dentifresh national launch sales conference, '...today, outside in the car park, on the roof of each of your cars has been fixed a giant tube of Dentifresh. And this, gentlemen, is it....' Dramatically he pulled aside a black cloth, uncovering a statue of a toothpaste tube about four feet high, on which was written big, bold and bright:

DENTIFRESH
Brushes Dentures Clean
And Your Own Teeth Too

The sales manager waited for the polite applause which habitually follows the unveiling of such displays at sales conferences. There was silence. Disconcerted, he continued: 'Now we are not going to *force* any of you to keep these Dentifresh tubes on your cars...'

A sales rep's free car is his pride and joy, his major perk; parked outside of his semi it constitutes his finest display of conspicuous wealth. It is the symbol of his affluence, the icon which keeps him a radiator grille ahead of the Jones's. It is not an object on which to display massive denture cleansing toothpaste tubes.

'...but this is your way of showing your enthusiasm for this really great product you've been given to sell today. Gentlemen, Dentifresh is a product we here are all going to be very proud of. This evening we are all going to drive through town in a cavalcade, with our Dentifresh tubes proudly displayed on our car roofs. After that you can, I'm saying you *can*, take your tube down, if you feel you must. But, gentlemen, I can tell you they are pretty firmly fixed, ha ha! And I don't mind saying that we in management, we're not saying you've got to keep your Dentifresh tubes up, because when you joined the company each of you was given your car as it is, and we're not going back on that. I'm just saying if any of you does take the tube off we will be very, very disappointed in you. *Very* disappointed. Over the next few weeks we want you to tour the country, showing the chemists and grocers, how much you believe in Dentifresh. Now . . .' he looked menacingly around the hall trying to sound as threatening as his normally kind and friendly voice would allow, 'now, if there is any one of you, and I'm sure there won't be, who is going to *disappoint* us, if there is any one of you who wants to take the Dentifresh tube off his car after the cavalcade this evening, let him stand up. Let's all see him. . . .'

Nobody rose.

'Well, there you are,' the sales manager hurried quickly on, 'there you are, you've all justified my confidence in you.'

At that moment one of the reps stood up. He was a huge man, tough as a rhino and known for his belligerence. 'I don't want it on my car,' he said loudly, 'and I'm not having it neither.'

Within sixty seconds almost every other rep in the hall was on his feet in defiant rebellion.

That was the second sales conference insurrection I have witnessed. The first was a more gentlemanly affair. The Save and Prosper Group employed retired high-ranking officers from the armed services, to call on professional financial advisers—stockbrokers, bank managers, solicitors and accountants. The ingenious idea was that such men, all of whom were intelligent and extremely conscientious, would work part-time and without supervision for a comparatively low salary to supplement their service pensions. They were called consultants rather than sales representatives. And no bank manager or accountant could possibly refuse to see a chap whose visiting card read:

H. L. Fortescue-Smyth, D.F.C.
Wing Commander (Retd)
Consultant.

Shortly after Tom Stewart came from Procter and Gamble as Marketing Comptroller to the Save and Prosper Group, he decided that splendid as these worthy men were, they were being allowed a little too much freedom to do and say what they liked. He felt that they constituted an undeveloped resource, a team which with a little gentle training could be far more effective.

His first move was to produce a salesman's portfolio. Just the normal plastic folder which most sales representatives carry. Such portfolios are intended to form the backbone of each sales presentation, detailing the items being sold in the order in which they should be shown. Aware that his proposal might raise the consultants' hackles, Tom had produced very expensive, very distinguished portfolios to which not even the most sensitive rear admiral (retd) could take offence.

Unfortunately Tom had forgotten that one of the consultants had only one good arm. When shown the beautiful portfolio at the sales conference, this man firmly insisted that with only one active hand it would be impossible for him to carry such a thing, much as he admired it. The other consultants all commiserated with him, and immediately each thought of his own reason why he was unable to use the portfolio.

The portfolios were never used.

The main difficulty about sales conferences is that they are never sufficiently well rehearsed. Grand sales conferences, which may cost as much as £30,000, are intended to be something half-way between a three-ring circus and a general's pep-talk to the troops before battle. Unfortunately the businessmen involved in the conference are, in the nature of things, usually too busy to arrive in advance and rehearse. And, again in the nature of things, most of the props and stage business do not arrive at the conference until the eleventh hour. At best there will be one quick run-through the day before. Fortunately most businessmen are reasonably adept at public speaking, and can ad-lib adequately when things go wrong as, in the nature of things, they regularly do.

The sensible way to plan sales conferences is take account of the fact that there is unlikely ever to be a full dress rehearsal. Avoid unnecessarily complicated machinery: it will break. (At the otherwise highly successful launch conference for Admiral, Norman Griffiths attempted to build up an eight-foot-high reproduction of the Press ad on a huge vertical magnetic board, piece by piece like a jigsaw. The magnets were not strong enough. The pieces slithered around. Arms appeared from behind the magnetic board, as if from a Javanese dance goddess, holding the pieces in place.) Avoid rapid and frequent changes of medium—slides to film to telecine to slides to film; avoid rapid cross-talk between speakers. Very obvious advice, forgotten repeatedly and disastrously.

The prime task of the speaker from the ad agency is to persuade the sales force that the forthcoming advertising will be the heaviest/most powerful/most impactful campaign ever run; so that each sales rep can in turn persuade the retailers that the forthcoming advertising will be the heaviest/most powerful/most impactful campaign ever run—and that the retailer had better stock up or he will lose tens of millions of customers to the shop down the road.

Almost invariably the sales manager compering the conference will introduce the speaker from the ad agency by the wrong name. I have been announced as Winston Smith, Winston Graham, Howard Winston and Jack Clark. In all probability the sales manager will also get the agency's name wrong and the speaker's job title too. It is desirable not to be disconcerted by this mêlée of blunders.

Most agency men, and indeed most marketing men, treat the sales force as naïve simpletons. They talk down to the reps, condescendingly calling them 'gentlemen' or 'you lads', telling well-worn dirty jokes (jokes are, remember, a salesman's stock in trade), and repeating tired clichés. Most reps

go to at least two conferences a year, so that by the age of
fifty they may have attended sixty or more conferences.
Regularly at each conference, and at every new product
launch, the reps have been promised the heaviest/most
powerful/most impactful campaign ever run. The reps see
products come and go, and but a handful of them succeed. A
salesman's life is a lonely one; it breeds hardy cynicism and
an independent mind.

At each new product launch, the sales force are invoked
'to help create and share in the success of this exciting new
venture'. I await the day when one of the reps shouts back,
'OK, so I'll help to create the success; how will I share in it?'

As well as communicating his simple message, the agency
man is often expected to be the day's clown. Having listened
patiently and sleepily to the sales manager, the production
manager, the brand manager, the marketing manager and
one or two other uninspiring managers, the sales reps look
forward eagerly to the agency man's turn. They anticipate a
little light relief.

Pity then the poor ad man who is no extrovert, no would-be
Thespian raconteur; who wishes merely to say his piece as
quickly, simply and undramatically as possible. For any ad
man whose natural inclination is to lock himself in the lavatory whenever he hears at a party the dreaded word charade,
who is only too happy to find a bushel under which to hide
his light, here are six simple tricks to perform when forced
to do so at sales conferences:

The Funny Fiver: 'Now here is a fiver' (wave fiver in air).
'Because this is such an important day for us all, I feel that
we should mark it in some way. Now, is there anyone in the
hall whose birthday it is today? You, sir? Are you sure it's
your birthday today? You swear it? Well then, may I say to
you "happy birthday". Many, many happy returns.' (Pocket
fiver.) Much laughter from rest of audience.

If nobody admits to a birthday, ask whether it is the birthday of the wife of any one of them. If it's nobody's wife's
birthday, give up this joke and hurry on.

The Fiver For Real (particularly effective immediately after The Funny Fiver): 'Now you've all seen the television schedule. Thirty second peak-time spots on every station in the country. Now here is a fiver which I'll give to anyone who can guess to within ten the total number of spots going out all over the country during this great campaign.' (This time the fiver *must* be given to the winner.)

Equally effective for the number of readers reached by a Press schedule or its total circulation, or just about anything arithmetical and guessable.

The Deliberately Mistaken Fiver (only usable at the conference immediately subsequent to The Fiver For Real): 'Now you'll all remember that last time I was here I gave a fiver to...' (It is important here to get the name right.) 'This time I've got another money prize, a *mysterious* money prize here in my top pocket' (pat top pocket). 'Today I shall make a deliberate mistake, and whoever spots it will win the mystery money prize. Are you ready?'

(Very important with this one to try to make only one mistake during the speech. If depressing history has taught you that you are bound to make several mistakes, this whole ploy is best avoided.) The mystery money prize, surprise, surprise, is ½p.

Bring on The Dancing Girls (this one, in which Mark Ramage was particularly dashing, requires a little more time and organization): 'I know that not all of you like the ads we run for...' (It is important here to remember which company you are addressing.) 'But the fact is, you can't please all of the people all of the time. And ads are a bit like girls. One man's Sleeping Beauty is another's Ugly Sister. To prove my point I'm going to hold a little beauty competition here, now, and bring on six bathing beauties. You will have to judge them—listen to this carefully—in the order from one to six that you think will get most votes. *Not* necessarily the order that you yourself prefer. But the order you think your colleagues here in the room will choose. Because that's the advertising business. *Not* choosing the ads which please you yourself but the ads you think will please—and persuade —the public.' The girls, hired from a model agency, then make their entrance dressed in as few clothes as you think the client company will wear, as it were, to happy jeers and catcalls from the auditorium. A jolly time is had by all. If anyone guesses the order right—and the odds against are 720 to 1, so you should be safe unless it is a mammoth sales force—you'll have to award a prize. Possibly dinner with one of the girls.

(This one has a relevant moral for the client's marketing department, which invariably will be ignored.)

Bring on The Dancing Girls, Economy Size: Exactly the same, but substituting photographs of the girls on slides. This is cheaper and quicker but much less fun.

Congratulations, Have a Cigar (this comes out expensive with sales forces of more than fifty men): Once again a simple quiz is conducted—I'm a great enthusiast for audience participation—preferably one with questions which reward any rep who may have had the kindness and concentration to listen to your speech. The winner is declared, and you say, 'Congratulations. Now I happened to know in advance, being of a psychic disposition, that you would be the winner. And, therefore, stuck underneath the seat of your chair you will find your prize—a fine, fat, Havana cigar.' Thereupon the winner searches under his chair and does indeed find a fine, fat, Havana cigar. All are amazed at your clairvoyant power, and the applause may be deafening. Little do they know that under every chair is a fine, fat, Havana cigar. Unfortunately almost inevitably one of them guesses. Then in a trice all of them are down on their knees searching for their undeserved prizes. The curtain falls on the pandemonium.

Sales conferences should be fun. They also tend to be occasions when everyone drinks more than somewhat, and a certain amount of *in vino veritas* between client and agency may ensue. Handled delicately, this can be very useful to the agency man, providing he can restrain himself from coming on strong with too much *veritas* of his own. Where else but at a sales conference would I have learned that Dennis Ing was no Eskimo?

It was at a sales conference that I received the only indecent proposition I have ever had from a client. It was one o'clock in the morning and a brand manager and myself were propping up the hotel bar, which had of course closed for everyone except residents.

'Why don't,' he said generously, 'you and your wife come and stay with me and my wife one weekend?'

'Why not?'

'Why not?'

Our capacity to move the conversation along quickly and wittily had long been impaired.

'When?' I asked.

'You know what I mean?'

'When?' I repeated.

'I mean we're very friendly, me and my wife. You know what I mean?'

'Whaddyou mean?'

'I mean we're very friendly. You know the kind of thing?'

In a more lucid moment I feel that I might have known the kind of thing. 'Whaddyou mean?'

'I mean if your wife takes a fancy to me....'

'She won't.'

He had never met my wife who was, at the time, seven months pregnant. This fact had not before crept into the conversation because it had not seemed relevant.

'How do you know she won't?' he asked, hurt.

'I don't know. I just know I know. Anyway what happens if your wife takes a fancy to me? Or vice versa?'

'Whaddyou mean vice versa?' he asked quickly, perhaps scenting some new twist he had not previously come across.

'I mean vice versa. If I fancy her I mean.'

'You like blondes or brunettes?'

'Don't care.'

'My wife looks Jewish. She's not, though. People think she is, though. Ever had a Jewish girl?'

'Did I tell you my wife's pregnant?'

'Boy or girl?'

'She's a girl. That's usual.'

'Oh.' He looked at me contemplatively, whisky glazing his eyes. 'Then you won't wanna come and stay with us, then.'

'Suppose not.'

It's the only naughty proposition of the kind I've had in fifteen years of advertising, much as I mix with housing-estate executives and their sometimes over-affectionate wives. Either those who participate keep their activities very secret or there is much less hanky-panky going on than the Permissive Society would have us believe.

14   A Day Out with One of
the Boys

Lying in bed the night before a field trip I invariably regret
the whole thing. The prospect of spending a full day calling
on wholesalers and retailers, in the company of a nervous
sales rep who suspects that the secret purpose of my trip
is to spy on him, begins to depress me deeply. I lie thinking
of all the work I should be doing at my office desk, remembering all the unwritten reports I should be writing, desperately wishing that I had never agreed to catch, at the cold
crack of dawn, a train to one of the drearier Midlands industrial towns. No matter how self-assured you are, the prospect of spending a day in the close company of somebody
you have never met before must always be slightly disturb-
ing.

Climbing from the train you scan the waiting crowd for a
man whose inadequate description you were given hurriedly
on the telephone the evening before. To help you identify
him he will probably be carrying your client's product—a
bottle of Justina perhaps or a packet of Kleenex tissue—holding it up awkwardly and embarrassedly to ensure that you
notice him. You walk with him to his car making small talk,
eyeing him a little nervously. The full realization slowly
dawns that you are going to spend eight hours together; that
quite probably you are going to dislike his politics, his pre-
tensions, his tastes, his life-style, the colour pictures of his
children that he will proudly show you and the carping
criticisms of his company that he will—cautiously at first,
but steadily growing bolder—almost inevitably express.

Lying in bed the night before, the prospect seems deplorable. Less than twenty-four hours later, enjoying a drink on

the train back to town and meditating on the day's events, I realize how extremely worthwhile it has all been. There is no better way to learn quickly and accurately what is happening in the marketplace—how well or badly your own and your competitors' products are selling, and why—than by spending a day out with one of the boys.

My first field trip took me no further afield than Islington. Not yet knowing what the form was, I expected the day to be a jolly skive, and dressed accordingly. I was accompanying a rep for Claytons, a small London based soft-drink company since acquired by Beechams. The rep was selling mixers and squashes to pubs. You need a good strong liver to sell things to pubs.

Our first call was at ten-thirty, and the publican offered us a half-of-bitter.

'It's a bit early, isn't it?' I whispered to the rep.

'Unfriendly to refuse,' he whispered back. 'All part of the job.'

We downed our beers, and the rep bought us all the other half. 'Always return the compliment,' he whispered, 'or you'll never get another order.'

'Should I buy a round too?' I asked him still in a whisper, as the second round of halves quickly disappeared.

'You'd better. He thinks you're from Claytons, so he'll expect you to buy him one.'

We left the pub at about eleven o'clock. By one o'clock we had visited four more gloomy pubs in Clerkenwell, Finsbury, Canonbury and Hoxton, virtuously drinking one-and-a-half pints in each. I was sloshed.

'We'd better have something to eat,' my leader said, 'settle our tum-tums.'

I had not previously considered the lunch problem. What class of restaurant should we go to? Who should pay for whom? Should we each pay for ourselves?

'What do you usually do for lunch when you're on your own?' I asked hesitantly.

The rep looked at me coldly. Tradition, I have since learned, dictates that the agency man buys the rep a reasonably good lunch as a gesture of gratitude. Seasoned reps are well aware of this tradition.

'I usually have a sausage, on one of my calls.'

I sensed that he was expecting a somewhat grander repast on this occasion, but I had not the least idea where we might feast in Hoxton; moreover, unprepared for the situation and having already bought seven-and-a-half pints of bitter, I had only a couple of quid left on me.

'I wouldn't mind a sausage,' I said warmly. 'On a stick. With mustard.'

'Will that be enough for you?' There was a distinct note of asperity in his voice.

'I might have a scotch egg too. And potato salad. Do the pubs round here have scotch eggs and potato salad?'

'No.'

'Well ... just have to have sausages then. I like a good pork sausage.'

I paid for the sausages. We drank more beer, and then carried on our rounds until three o'clock when the pubs shut.

'They don't like you calling after three,' he warned me. 'Most of them take their forty winks in the afternoon.'

We had called on eight pubs in all, I think, and had each drunk about twelve pints of bitter. It was in the days before the breathalyser, but Heaven alone knows how he was still managing to drive adequately.

We drank a cup of tea in a café somewhere in Hackney, and at about four o'clock I staggered off home and to sleep. Apart from the awkward incident of the lunch, I felt that we had spent a pleasant, friendly day together. I had not drunk so much for so long since my post-examination days at Cambridge.

I sent him a nice thank-you letter the next day, and wrote a long report detailing what I had learnt—or rather what I could remember—for Clayton's management.

Three days later I was severely reprimanded. I had insulted the rep and caused him great embarrassment by turning up for the trip *improperly dressed*. Apparently his day had been one long torment, as I had been wearing unbusinesslike suède shoes and had been indecently exposing a hatless head.

Things are a little easier now. Reps no longer wear hats as

symbols of their respectability. Nevertheless they are rightly very conscious of the impression they create, and are today extremely unhappy at being accompanied by long-haired young men dressed, as they think untidily and garishly. Since virtually 100 per cent of the young men employed in ad agencies and in marketing companies look totally disreputable, by reps'—and for that matter by most retailers'—standards, this causes difficulties.

I remember gently suggesting to a young account executive that before going out for a day visiting chemists, he might get his hair trimmed, just a little.

He was most indignant. 'I'm not changing my appearance just to please small-minded bourgeois shopkeepers,' he replied forcefully. 'They don't grow their hair longer when the boot's on the other foot and I go in to buy a bottle of aspirin.'

Nowadays I aim to go on a field trip for each of my clients at least once a year and preferably twice. This involves, in total, many days every year away from the office; which could be thought to be a waste of time. Obviously I do not agree. As I grow older and more experienced, if not necessarily wiser, I learn more and more from each trip. Textbooks tell you that field trips are a good way to check on your products' distribution level. This is usually nonsense. In one day you will not have time to visit properly more than a dozen shops, and these will anyway have been selected for you by the rep. Hardly a random sample.

Field trips provide what market researchers call 'soft data': non-statistical insights, gossip about competitors' activity, trade reactions (important, if unreliable) to your consumer advertising and promotions. Above all, if you incessantly ask questions, take copious detailed notes, and stay totally alert, you absorb an atmospheric sense of what is happening. I have never spent a day in the field and felt it wasted.

Field trips can be a little dangerous. Particularly during test markets. Many retailers do not like test markets. They feel that in a test market the retailer is used as a guinea pig

and shoulders most of the financial risk. There is some justification for this feeling. The manufacturer, uncertain of the
success of a new product, limits his risk by testing it in one
small area of the country. The retailer has every right to be
equally uncertain of the product's success—but he is unable
to limit his risk similarly. If the product fails, the manufacturer will cut his losses while the retailer will be left with
dead stock. The manufacturer may agree to take the unsold
stock back, at a price, or he may not. In theory, retailers
too benefit in the long run from test marketing, which results
in fewer dud products being launched nationally. A retailer
in Lancashire who loses on product X gains in his turn at the
expense of a retailer in Yorkshire who loses on product Y;
without test marketing, both might have lost on both.

The fallacy in this logic, from the retailer's point of view, is
that some areas of the country are very frequently used as
test markets, others almost never. No one area of the country
is totally typical of the rest, but Southern and Tyne-Tees
are the television areas most frequently used for tests. York
is one of the most used towns.

In York we test-marketed Limmits Slim-Meals—calorie-
controlled canned meals for slimmers. Each can contained a
complete, balanced, satisfying meal which, if eaten in place
of normal food, would positively help you slim. A few weeks
after the test market had started, together with Terry Clark,
then marketing director in charge of Limmits Slim-Meals, I
visited York on a tour of inspection. Every chemist we visited
reported gloomily that the product was sticking. Nonetheless, they were civil to us. Until we visited Timothy Whites.
I was suffering from an upset stomach, and was privately
sipping a draught to settle it when I suddenly realized that
Terry was being verbally savaged by a tall, gaunt man. Apparently this was the manager of the shop. 'Why do you come
here?' the man was shouting angrily as Terry backed away
from him. 'You're prostituting our city with your damn tests.
York's a depressed area. There's mass unemployment here.
We can't afford all your damn expensive new products and
your damn test markets. Why don't you leave us alone?'

I continued to drink my draught as if I were a customer

and in no way associated with Terry or his detestable test.

'We chose York because it's pretty typical of the country. You should be glad to get a crack at some of these profitable new lines before the rest of the country does,' Terry counter-attacked, though he was now almost out of the door.

'Typical?' yelled the gaunt man. 'Nonsense. York's not typical. Tell me this, then. Tell me this. Where in the country can you find more shoe shops than in York?'

It was a question to stymie even the nimblest mind.

'Luton,' Terry replied firmly.

His antagonist's jaw dropped. 'How did you know that?'

'That's the kind of thing chaps like you and I know,' Terry answered generously as he turned to leave the store and I scurried after him.

15   How to Get Yourself on Juke Box Jury

PR is something which always seems to go wrong. There are, no doubt, somewhere in the world skilful manipulators of the mass media; *éminences grises* in suits-to-match who cleverly plant a deadly rumour here, drop a devious word in the right ear there, exert arcane influence everywhere. Men who are as powerful and cunning in their PR world as the ad makers are in theirs. There are no doubt such people, but I have yet to meet them. Perhaps I have been unlucky.

'Hallo. Hallo. Is that *The Times*?' It was the PR man on the telephone in the next office. 'I want to speak to the editor of *The Times*. Yes, the editor.' Pause. 'Yes. That the editor's secretary? Can I speak to the editor, please? I'm managing director of Dover Street Public Relations ... Of course it's important ... I want to report a world record ... Isn't *The Times* interested in world records now? I'm giving you an exclusive here.' (Aside to his secretary with, I hope, his hand over the mouthpiece: 'No wonder their bloody circulation's falling like a stone. I've a good mind to ring off and give this one to the *Guardian*.') 'Yes, yes, a world record.... All right, then, I'll speak to the news editor. Yes. Thank you.... Is that the news editor? This is the managing director of Dover Street Public Relations. I want to report a world record. I'm giving it to you exclusive ... Yes ... Is that the news editor? At last. If you knew the troubles I've had getting through to you, I'm surprised you ever get any stories.... This is a world record. It could be a *Times* exclusive.... I've checked the facts. It's definitely a world record. Twenty-one students in a Morris 1100 for 30 minutes ... last night at Mitcham ... Whaddyou mean wasting your time? It's a world record...'

Advertising agencies should not own PR subsidiaries. There are many good reasons for this. The most important being that PR companies are high-risk and low-profit enterprises. High risks are endemic in the PR business because the human raw materials with which it works—journalists and television producers—are sceptical, obdurate people whose careers depend on them uncovering scandals and skeletons-in-cupboards, and who for the most part don't much like PRO's.

Profits are low because agencies are forced to pay those few good PR people that exist fairly high salaries, to dissuade them from leaving and opening their own shops. You need no capital to start a PR company. A garret in Fleet Street, a part-time secretary, a few hundred visiting cards, one of which is stuck with a drawing pin in the bell-push at the door —and you are established. If you have even a modicum of initiative and drive, why work for Lexington (JWT's PR subsidiary) or Planned Public Relations (Young and Rubicam's)? Unless they pay you a good deal more than you could make by doing your own thing. Moreover, if as a director of one of these agency PR subsidiaries you see it making vast and fat profits, what greater incentive could there be to persuade you to leave, maybe taking with you a couple of accounts to which you have personally become attached?

Public Relations is a living contradiction of the Marxist Labour Theory of Surplus Value: there being no capital involved, all surplus value accrues to the workers, and the capitalists cannot effectively get their greedy hands on it. It is unfortunately doubtful whether Marx would have considered that PR men were workers, and he would therefore no doubt have discounted this argument.

Thus, what with cut-price competition from one-man bands and the need to pay salaried employees highly, there is not much profit in it for an advertising agency. But the risks are especially great. There is always a fair possibility that you will lose a £500,000 advertising account because you have taken on the same client's PR at a fee of maybe £5,000 and some fool PR man makes a booboo with the chairman's annual statement.

A PR race was organized from Hyde Park Corner to Balham between an MG car, someone using public transport, and a penny-farthing bicycle. After protracted discussion it was agreed that in order to ensure maximum publicity, the penny-farthing should be ridden by a Very Famous Celebrity.

The Very Famous Celebrity, attired in full Victorian Sherlock Holmes gear, to the accompaniment of cheers and flash bulbs was launched bravely towards Balham from the centre of Hyde Park Corner. Unfortunately nobody had checked that he could ride a penny-farthing. He couldn't. The machine crashed on its side. The VFC tried again, crashed again, hailed a taxi and departed the scene.

I have never attended a successful Press conference. I mean successful in terms of results. I have attended several that were well organized and well attended. But even those failed to generate much publicity. The concept of the Press conference may work reasonably well in politics, where all the world is thought to be agog to hear even the tritest statement from our Leaders. But in business, most Press conferences are otiose.

Once upon a time perhaps, trade magazines and business papers published every puff PR handout that companies gave them. They still fail to exercise sufficient healthy scepticism and allow top businessmen to bamboozle them with half-truths and self-aggrandizing statements. But even the dimmest trade magazines have slowly come to realise that if they hope to be bought and read they must provide news, preferably exclusive news, which their competitor trade mags are not carrying. This is precisely the opposite of what Press conferences offer them.

The saddest Press conference I have ever attended was for

the launch of a new range of cosmetics. It was held at lunch
time on the top floor of the Royal Garden Hotel one sunny
summer's day. There was champagne, delicious food, and an
entrancing view out over Kensington Gardens and across
London. But there were no guests. There was a surfeit of
hosts, as ever. A dozen or so from the cosmetics company,
five of us from the ad agency. We drank many glasses of
champagne. Someone knocked over the massive glittering display of glossy new lipsticks and eye make-up scattering them
across the floor. The poor PR lady who had organized it
all was on the verge of tears.

Eventually a representative of the Press turned up. From
Ad Weekly.

I was taken, by a charming PRO I shall call Algernon, to a
publicity event where—after preliminary rounds at universi-
ties throughout the country—the final one of the many Miss-
Great-Britain Beauty Competition for Students was taking
place. There were six finalists, each from a different university.
They all seemed nice enough girls though by no means wond-
rously beautiful.

Algernon was backing one of them, whom we'll call Rita.
'It's all fixed,' he whispered to me. 'I've fixed it. Rita will win.
Watch.'

'How can you have fixed it?'

'Money, my boy. Bread. A few quid changed hands, and
it's fixed.'

'But...' The judges were three Extraordinarily Famous
(and rich) Celebrities. I couldn't believe that any of them
would accept a bribe. Certainly not a bribe of a few quid.
'But, Algernon, you can't possibly have bribed the judges.
Surely you haven't?'

'Just watch, boy. You'll see. I've got it fixed. And listen.
Clap as loud as you can every time Rita walks on. So it won't
look funny when she wins. She'd win anyway, mind you,
from what I've seen of the other five.'

The six girls appeared in their bathing costumes, walking
self-consciously and a little gauchely up the aisle to the judges'

table. They chatted to each of the judges in turn. The compère announced that as this was a university girls' competition their brains as well as their beauty were being taken into account. The judges marked them and the slips were collected.

The girls returned fully clothed, pirouetting and curtseying, smiling fixedly with counterfeited glee at everyone in sight. The compère announced that this time they were being judged for their dress sense and for grace. I dutifully clapped Rita loudly, although it was obvious that she was not one of the most attractive of the six. I would have placed her fourth or fifth. The judges' marked slips were collected again.

The girls returned and chatted nervously with the compère into the microphone. This was apparently a test of their personality. None of them seemed too strong in that department. The judges' slips were collected for the last time, and the compère announced a tension-heightening interval to give time for the marks to be counted and for us all to spend some money in the bar

Algernon was itching for the results to be declared and refused to go to the bar. 'Rita wins this,' he whispered, 'and we're made. She's cut the disc already. We'll release it—I'm her manager, boy—I'll get her on Jack de Manio and a couple of chat programmes. That's it. How d'you think they made Engelbert Humperdinck?'

'Did he win a Miss-Great-Britain Beauty Competition?'

Algernon was in no mood for banter. 'Sssh,' he said, 'sssh, the judges are coming back. This is it, boy.'

After the usual nonsensical preamble the compère announced, his voice suitably tremulous with excitement, the winner of the third prize in the Miss-Great-Britain Beauty Competition for Students. Then, tra-la-la tra-la-la, the second. And finally, here at last, ladies and gentlemen, it gives me really great pleasure to announce the moment you've all been waiting for, a truly wonderful moment for everyone of us here tonight, a beautiful girl and a worthy winner, here she is, tra-la-la tra-la-la, the lovely Miss Students-of-Great-Britain herself!

It was not Rita.

It was the girl who most deserved to win. She was the prettiest, had the best figure, the pleasantest personality and for all I know—since it *was* a university girls' competition—the highest IQ in the room.

Algernon was distraught. 'Somebody's fixed it,' he said, prim with moral outrage. 'Some bastard's kicked back a few more quid than me and done me.'

'But she was the obvious winner,' I said.

'Winner nothing. Boy, I had it fixed. So someone's outfixed me.'

'I told you all along you couldn't bribe Extraordinarily Famous Celebrities with a few quid,' I told-you-so'd him.

'Course not. Don't be a shmuck. You don't fix the judges. You fix the guy who adds the score up. Or one of the guys who collects the marking slips. A little change in the figures or an arithmetical slip, and who should know? But someone's done me.'

Beautiful. What simplicity! For the first time I understood why the judges at Olympic competitions hold their marks up on big white cards so that they can be seen throughout the hall. I had thought it was for the television cameras.

Suddenly Rita was running towards us. She was crying hysterically. She threw herself at Algernon, fiercely punching and pummelling his large chest. 'You...' she sobbed, 'you ... you've ruined me. You sod. You said you'd fix it. I didn't even ... not even third. She had fat legs too, that fucking girl.... I expect she had been on her back for all of them....'

'Never mind,' I said consolingly. 'Who wants to win a bloody silly contest like this? It was all just a PR stunt, anyway.'

I felt that she, as a university girl, could be expected to have some sense of the fatuousness of it all.

'Never mind?' she wailed, turning her attack from Algernon to me. 'Never mind? Don't you realize,' she was screaming by now, 'that if I'd bloodywell won I'd have been on JUKE BOX JURY?'

She was, indeed, a university girl.

There are a few PRO's in glamorous stainless steel and leather offices; no doubt they are friends of Cabinet Ministers and dine each night at Wiltons Oyster Bar. But most PR men do a steady, unglamorous job producing house magazines and issuing Press releases. Their pay is not wonderful, their influence is not, in my experience, very great. Their world is a rather drab, hard-working, ineffectual one. It is a world of executive swivel chairs with frayed fabric padding, of inexpensive Italian restaurants and mussel shells.

16   Are Ad Agencies Really
        Necessary?

The first known advertisements appeared in Pompeii in 3,000
B.C. Around 100 B.C. the Romans were heavy advertisers of
their games. The first advertisement in an English newspaper appeared in the *Newes* in 1622, and by 1657 Needham,
the enterprising editor of the *Publick Advertiser*, was charging
for advertisements according to the value of the items advertised.* By 1792 advertisements were 'the main support
and chief source of profit of newspapers as well as the most
natural channel of communication between the buyers and
sellers, the needing and supplying members of a vast com-
munity'.†

Probably the first advertising agent the world has ever
known started trading in London in 1812, Samuel Deacon &
Company. Throughout the nineteenth century the prime function of advertising agents was media broking. Ad agents were
paid commission by the media for selling space; but they
also collected data on the media so that they could
advise advertisers on where to spend their money most
effectively. Thus from the earliest days agents owed a dual
allegiance—to the media and to their clients. Agents charged
heftily for their services. Volnay B. Palmer, who founded the
first US agency in 1841, charged a wholesome 25 per-cent
commission.

By the 1850's a booklet entitled *Guide To Advertisers*
was going the rounds in London, compiled by 'An Old

---

* *History of Advertising* by Philippe Schuwer, published by Edito-Service,
S.A. Geneva, 1966.

† *A History of Advertising from the Earliest Times* by Henry Sampson,
Chatto and Windus, 1875.

Advertiser' who was 'desirous of imparting to other advertisers the results of his long and dearly bought experience'. Particularly, it seems, at the hands of disreputable people calling
themselves Advertising Agents. He added for his readers'
benefit, a list of 'respectable, responsible and established Advertising Agents with whom advertisers can safely deal' including C. Barker, C. Mitchell (now Mitchell Murray Phelan)
and C. & E. Layton.* But, until the turn of the last century,
manufacturers wrote and designed their own advertisements
—and amazing some of them were.†

The full service agency, which makes the advertisements
that fill the space it sells, did not come into existence even
in the United States until the 1890's. When Albert Lasker
joined Lord and Thomas in 1898 he found only one copywriter and one artist in the 'agency'. Lasker saw immediately
that an agency could only establish itself solidly with a client
by offering a high quality of creative service. He filled his
agency with ad makers; and the success of his approach can
be measured by the fact that six years later in 1904 he himself was earning $52,000 a year at Lord and Thomas.

In a house ad for his agency, Albert Lasker offered not
merely a Designing Department and an Advertisement Writing Department but also a Printing Department: clearly a
runaway USP at the time. George Batten—one of the found-
ers of BBDO—countered with sheer quality: 'What I have,'
his 1893 house-ad said simply, 'is of the best. My work is well
done. You know how hard it is to get any delicate work well
done.'

Because agencies started out by selling advertising space
for media and only later thought of producing the ads,
agencies are still paid by media rather than by advertisers
themselves. Agencies and advertisers frequently deny this
and say that *really* they are paid by the advertisers, and only
in theory are they paid by the media. This is simply not

---

* *A History of English Advertising* by Blanche B. Elliott, Business
Publications Ltd., 1962.
† The best are to be found in *Victorian Advertising* by Leonard de
Vries, published by John Murray, 1968.

true (except in the sense that when you buy a packet of corn-flakes you're paying for *Coronation Street*).

If a manufacturer goes to any national newspaper or magazine or to any local newspaper (except the very smallest) or to any commercial television company, he will be forced to pay, say, £100 for his space or time. If he goes to a recognized agency he will still pay £100 but the agency will pay the media only £85, taking its 15 per-cent commission on the way. Advertising agencies are thus employed by manufacturers but paid by the media. (This situation is not unique: the same is true of insurance brokers, for example.)

British media at present pay agencies a total of about £60 million a year (this is 15 per cent of the estimated volume of advertising placed by them). In return for their commission, agencies have, at various times, offered either for nothing or at below true economic cost: advertising research, market research, public relations, package design, below-the-line promotions, exhibition-stand designs, experimental photography and marketing advice in the middle of the night.

They have existed with account executives and without; with creative departments and without; they have been small, unorganized, red-hot think-tanks and large, structured, red-taped conglomerates. There is no platonically ideal agency organization. Under the commission system agencies have thought of a myriad ways to spend their 15 per cent.

But what do the media get for their money? Ten years ago the Shawcross Commission on the Press examined rather shallowly and sketchily the possibility that media should stop paying agencies. They asked a panel of advertising agencies whether the commission system was a good thing. Not altogether surprisingly, the agencies came out strongly in its favour. The main advantages to the media, they pointed out, were:

(1) There are many thousands of advertisers but only about 400 agencies; media do not have to worry about the financial probity of unknown manufacturers or collect debts from them. Agencies— principals in law—do all this.

(2) The commission system ensures that it is in the interest of agencies, just as it is in the interest of media, to get manufacturers to spend more on advertising—theoretically at least through the production of better, more effective advertising.

The important fact to grasp about the ad makers in advertising agencies is that in some respects they are the least important cogs in the advertising machinery. The manufacturers spend about £400 million each year to advertise their products; the media receive £340 million each year—and as a result we enjoy a plethora of cheap and mostly excellent news and entertainment services. The £60 million difference is the cost of making the advertisements. It sounds a lot. Until you think of the hundreds of thousands of new ads that are made each year—for television, billboards, newspapers, cinemas, magazines, trade journals, shop windows, match-box covers and the rest. The average cost per ad is tiny.

Masius, Wynne-Williams, one of the very largest British agencies, answered the Shawcross Commission's question like this: 'Perhaps the chief advantage of the commission system is that, like so many British practices, it is historic.' Well, almost a century old. Masius, Wynne-Williams added: 'The commission system also encourages competition (among agencies) by improved service and discourages price-cutting.'

As a result of the lack of price competition, advertising agencies have performed a valuable catalytic role in helping British (and indeed world) industry to move from a production-oriented to a consumer-oriented view of life.

Agencies have been instrumental in the development of the techniques of economic mass-marketing—the essential background to the economics of scale now achieved in the production of most consumer products. They were able to do these things because they were tiny conglomerates—staffed with market researchers and exhibition designers and God-knows-whaters as well as with writers and artists and space buyers. Thus they have given manufacturers all kinds of marketing help and advice, often free.

The ad makers are by no means infallible manipulators of the public mind. By its nature, making advertisements involves a continuous striving to be different, to create new ideas, to find new solutions to old problems. Breaking new ground inevitably involves errors and bungles; and these are compounded by the unfortunate fact that not every ad maker is 100 per cent competent—any more than is every lawyer or doctor or general.

If I have perhaps dwelled too much upon the ad makers' bloomers this is partly a reaction to the innumerable books* and articles which portray advertising and ad men as unerring, calculating monsters. I have tried hard to demonstrate that they are anything but. More fundamentally, as I mentioned in the Introduction, I personally happen to see life as a series of adventitious events over which human beings— and certainly ad makers—have far less control than they like to believe.

Arguments about advertising and ad makers do tend to suffer grievously from *folie de grandeur*. If I manufactured patterned wallpaper for my living I would not expect aggressive people forever to be accusing me of devious malpractices, nor to keep asking me whether patterned wallpaper is really essential to The Meaning of Life.

Of course advertising is not essential, in the sense that education, medicine and the law are essential. Advertising is necessary merely in the way that soft toilet tissue and stainless steel blades and pretty dresses and patterned wallpaper are. They make life a little more pleasant; and advertising helps the economic machine which produces them to work a little more efficiently. About one per cent of the Gross National Product is spent on consumer-product advertising. If this produces one point one per cent in return, we ad makers are earning our keep.

---

* One of the latest and silliest is *Imagery of Power* by Fred Inglis, Heinemann Education Books, 1972.

Index